Is China Buying the World?

For Maeve

Peter Nolan

IS CHINA
BUYING THE
WORLD?

polity

First published in 2012 by Polity Press

Polity Press
65 Bridge Street
Cambridge CB2 1UR, UK

Polity Press
350 Main Street
Malden, MA 02148, USA

ISBN-13: 978-0-7456-6078-3

A catalogue record for this book is available from the British Library.

Typeset in 11 on 14 pt Adobe Sabon
by Servis Filmsetting Ltd, Stockport, Cheshire
Printed and bound in the United States by Edwards Brothers

The publisher has used its best endeavours to ensure that the URLs for external websites referred to in this book are correct and active at the time of going to press. However, the publisher has no responsibility for the websites and can make no guarantee that a site will remain live or that the content is or will remain appropriate.

Every effort has been made to trace all copyright holders, but if any have been inadvertently overlooked the publisher will be pleased to include any necessary credits in any subsequent reprint or edition.

For further information on Polity, visit our website: www.politybooks.com

Contents

Contents

List of Tables

List of Tables

Acknowledgements

This book is based on a paper delivered to the board of the US–China Business Council in Washington, DC, on 1 June 2011. I am grateful to John Thompson both for his suggestion to turn this paper into a short book for a wider audience and for his close involvement in all aspects of the book's publication. I am grateful to Jin Zhang (Judge Business School, University of Cambridge) for her meticulous comments on the draft manuscript and to Bob Ash (School of Oriental and African Studies, London University), Vaclav Smil (University of Manitoba) and Ed Steinfeld (MIT) for their comments on the original paper.

Introduction

China's rise has astonished and mesmerized the public in the high-income countries.[1]

In 1990 China's GDP (at market prices) was just 1.6 per cent of the world total and it was the world's eleventh largest economy. By 2008 its share of world GDP had increased to 7.1 per cent and it had risen to become the world's third largest economy (World Bank, 2006, 2010). If national output is measured in 'purchasing power parity' dollars instead of using market prices, then China's share of total world output is 11.4 per cent and it is the world's second largest economy. Indeed, using this measure, China's gross national income is already 54 per cent of that of the USA (World Bank, 2010). China's GDP growth rate in the past two decades has been over 10 per cent per annum compared with less

---

[1] One should, more correctly, speak of China's 'renaissance'. Before the European Industrial Revolution China was by far the world's largest economy, with an estimated one-third of total global output of goods and services, far above that of Europe until the nineteenth century.

than 3 per cent in the high-income economies.[2] If things continue in this fashion, China's GDP will soon exceed that of the USA.

China's rise is a puzzle for most commentators. The central proposition of the 'transition orthodoxy', espoused by self-designated transition experts such as Jeffrey Sachs, Anders Aslund and Janos Kornai, was the incompatibility of the Communist Party with a market economy (Nolan, 1995). For the 'transition orthodoxy', this was the lesson that China should have learned from the USSR and Eastern Europe: 'The collapse of communist one-party rule was the sine qua non for an effective transition to a market economy. If one proposition has been tested by history, it is that the communist parties of Eastern Europe would not lead a process of reform sufficiently deep to create a real market economy' (Lipton and Sachs, 1990).[3] To the amazement of the mainstream view, China's economy has prospered beyond imagination under the rule of the Chinese Communist Party, which now has over 80 million members and has just celebrated its ninetieth anniversary. Following the collapse of the Communist Party of the Soviet Union, the economy and society disintegrated, with huge suffering for the mass of the population. The contrast between 'China's

[2] Unless otherwise indicated, this book follows the World Bank's classification of countries into 'high-income' (those with a Gross National Income per person at market prices of $11,906) and 'low- and middle-income' countries below this level (World Bank, 2010: xxiii).

[3] The forgetfulness of the 'transition experts' is reminiscent of the character in Samuel Beckett's monologue *Not I*, which was written for Billie Whitelaw. In the short play she describes her awful life and periodically punctuates the story with piercing cries of 'not I'.

rise' and 'Russia's fall' (Nolan, 1995) is one of the most significant issues in modern world history.

There is constant discussion of China in the international mass media and an avalanche of publications on different aspects of China's rise. The over-riding sentiment in both Europe and the USA is fear. This is reflected in the titles of the best-selling books on China, such as Martin Jacques's *When China Rules the World: The Rise of the Middle Kingdom and the End of the Western World* (2009), Stefan Halper's *Beijing Consensus: How China's Authoritarian Model Will Dominate the Twenty-First Century* (2010) and Arvind Subramaniam's *Eclipse: Living in the Shadow of China's Economic Dominance* (2011). The fears are comprehensive, covering all aspects of the relationship with China.

The profoundly fearful sentiments on America's Capitol Hill are reflected in the US–China Economic and Security Review Commission, which was set up in October 2000 by the US Congress in order to 'monitor and investigate and report to Congress on the national security implications of the bilateral trade and economic relationship between the United States and the People's Republic of China'. The commissioners are all appointed by Congress. The commission has produced a succession of annual reports, each of which expresses deep apprehensions about the implications of China's economic rise for the United States, including the impact on US employment and conditions of work and upon the country's technological and military superiority. At one of its hearings Vice-Chairman C. Richard D'Amato commented:

If you can figure out how to integrate a Chinese communist dictatorship with over a billion people who go where they're told to go; who work in the industry they're told to told to work [in]; who get paid what they're told they're worth; who have no way to answer back, if you can figure out how to integrate that into the world economy, please let me know.

China's foreign exchange reserves have risen from relatively insignificant amounts to become by far the largest of any country. In the year 2000 China's foreign exchange reserves stood at just US$166 billion. After China joined the World Trade Organization (WTO) in 2001 its exports grew at high speed. By December 2006 its foreign exchange reserves had increased to $1,066 billion. By April 2009 they exceeded $2,000 billion, and by June 2011 they stood at $3,197 billion. China's foreign exchange reserves are now almost three times as large as those of Japan ($1,138 billion), which are in turn more than twice as large as those of the third-ranked country, Russia ($531 billion). China has become by far the largest foreign holder of US public debt. By June 2011 it held $1,170 billion of US Treasury bills, notes and bonds, compared with $911 billion for Japan, $350 billion for Britain and $230 billion for the oil-exporting countries. China accounted for 26 per cent of the total foreign holdings of US government debt.[4] This has aroused intense media discussion of the

---

[4] As well as foreign holders, domestic entities account for 52 per cent of total holdings of US public debt. In other words, China's share of total US public debt is only around 12 per cent. If all US government debt is included (publicly held and non-publicly held) its share falls even lower, to around 8 per cent. Moreover, Japan and Britain between them own more

implications of the USA's high level of indebtedness to its largest single creditor, China.

There is wide discussion in the high-income countries about the impact that the integration of China into the world economy has had upon real incomes, income distribution and conditions of work. In the United States it is argued that 'de-industrialization', stagnation of the median wage and increased inequality are closely linked with China's explosive growth of industrial output and exports.[5] China has over 950 million people of working age, compared with 720 million in all the high-income countries combined. China's exports of mainly labour-intensive products grew by 14 per cent per annum in the 1990s, accelerating to 25 per cent per annum after 2000. China is now deeply integrated into the world trading system. Its merchandise exports amount to 59 per cent of GDP, an exceptionally high figure, and three-quarters of its exports are to the high-income countries (World Bank, 2010).

There is deep fear in the United States that China's rise will transform fundamentally the balance of global military power. In the view of the US government, China is the one country that has the potential to challenge US supremacy. In 2002 President Bush warned:

US public debt than China – $1,261 billion compared with $1,170 billion. In per capita terms, Japanese and British holdings vastly exceed those of China.

[5] Between 1969 and 2009 the real average earnings of full-time US male workers aged sixteen to sixty-four were unchanged. However, due to the increase in part-time and short-term contracts, the total US median male real wage fell 28 per cent in the same period (*Financial Times*, 23 September 2011).

In pursuing advanced military capabilities that can threaten its neighbours in the Asia-Pacific region, China is following an outdated path that, in the end, will hamper its own pursuit of greatness. It is time to reaffirm the essential role of American military strength. We must build and maintain our defences beyond challenge . . . Our forces will be strong enough to dissuade potential adversaries from pursuing a military build-up in hopes of surpassing, or equalling, the power of the US.

The Pentagon's *Quadrennial Defense Review* of 2006 stated: 'Of the major powers, China has the greatest potential to compete militarily with the United States and field disruptive military technologies that could over time offset traditional US military advantages absent [*sic*] counter strategies.'

There are deep fears also across the high-income countries concerning China's impact upon the values that will govern the global community in the years ahead. There is wide agreement among Western politicians and analysts that Western 'Enlightenment' principles should form the foundation for the world's value system in the twenty-first century. Stefan Halper, who served in the White House under successive Republican administrations, considers that these principles 'represent a basic agreement, resting on the consent of the governed and committing government to ensure the rights of speech, belief, assembly, and political expression, provided it is peaceful, tolerant, and guided by compromise' (Halper, 2010: 249). In the view of Will Hutton, who is a leading British author, the West 'needs to stand by its values and institutions at home, and reproduce them internationally to give the rest of the world a genuine opportunity to catch up and to recast its domestic organisation around Enlightenment principles' (Hutton, 2007: 342). Subramaniam's book (2011) warns against the coming 'eclipse' in which the 'sun' of the Western Enlightenment will be blotted out by China's economic dominance and a 'shadow' will cover the Western world.

Western analysts from widely differing political persuasions have warned of the dangers posed by China's authoritarian development model, which they characterize as the 'Beijing Consensus'. Halper, for example, argues that: 'on matters of global ethics and governing principles America's voice – its most important asset – has been muted when it comes to China', and that it is in danger of 'surrendering the moral authority and Western inheritance that has animated America's appeal for two hundred years' (Halper, 2010: xii). He views the core ethics of the Chinese model as based on age-old 'Confucian values': 'Whereas the Western ruler has a responsibility to insure the people have the right of political expression, assembly, and the debate in the public square and the people have a duty to exercise those rights, the exact opposite is true in Confucian society' (ibid.: 250). He asks: 'How can Beijing can be a "responsible stakeholder", as World Bank President Robert Zoellick contends, while its policies enable systematic repression among its impoverished partners and erode the values now informing the international system?' (ibid.: xi).[6] Halper's book *Beijing Consensus*

---

[6] In 2006, the (then) US Deputy Secretary of State, Zoellick, proposed that the United States should try to work with China to become a 'responsible stakeholder' in the international system. In 1998 a group of eighteen leading US political figures, including Zoellick, signed a highly publicized

concludes with a 'clarion call' which urges America's leaders to engage in 'a global struggle to assert and sustain the primacy of Western values' (ibid.: 252).

In the last few years in the high-income countries there has developed a gathering hysteria over the perceived threat to human civilization from burning fossil fuels. In his apocalyptic book *Collapse* (2005), Jared Diamond paints a nightmare vision of the environmental implications for America consequent upon China's rise. In a new version of the 'Yellow Peril' view of China, he warns that the country's large population, economy and area 'guarantee that its environmental problems will not remain a domestic issue but will spill over to the rest of the world, which is increasingly affected through sharing the same planet, oceans, and atmosphere with China':

> China is already the largest contributor of chlorofluorocarbons, other ozone-depleting substances, and (soon) carbon dioxide to the atmosphere; its dust and aerial pollutants are transported eastwards in the atmosphere to neighbouring countries and even to North America; and it is one of the two leading importers of tropical rainforest timber, making it a driving force behind tropical deforestation.

Diamond argues that even more important than all those other impacts will be the 'proportionate increase in total human impact on the world's environment if

letter to President Clinton, urging him to act decisively to 'pre-empt Iraq's possible acquisition of weapons of mass destruction before it was too late'. Other signatories included Donald Rumsfeld, Paul Wolfowitz, Richard Perle and Francis Fukuyama.

China, with its large population, succeeds in its goal of achieving First World living standards – which also means catching up to the First World's environmental impact.' He believes that if China achieves First World living standards it will 'approximately double the entire world's human resource use and environmental impact'. He doubts whether even the world's current human resource use and impact can be sustained: 'Something has to give way. That is the strongest reason why China's problems automatically become the world's problems.' Diamond is concerned at yet another threat to the United States from China's rise:

> Still another species of which China has an abundant population, which has large ecological and economic impacts, and which China is exporting in increasing numbers, is Homo Sapiens. For instance, China has now moved into third place as a source of legal immigration into Australia and significant numbers of illegal as well as legal immigrants crossing the Pacific reach even the United States.

Among the numerous Western fears that have emerged is the concern that China's firms are 'buying the world'. Lurid headlines abound, such as *The Economist*'s cover story (November 2010) 'Buying up the world: The coming wave of Chinese takeovers' and *The Independent*'s cover story (*The Independent*, 2 October 2010) 'The great haul of China: As Beijing's spending spree extends to Brazil, what does it mean for the world?'. The cover story of *Fortune* magazine's edition of 26 October 2009 was captioned 'China buys the world': 'The Chinese have $2 trillion and are going shopping. Is your company – and your country – on their list?' The story inside the *Fortune* issue was entitled 'It's China's world (we just live in it)':

> The Chinese have long been on a shopping spree for natural resources. Now with $2 trillion in their pockets, they are shifting their aim toward auto-makers, high-tech firms, and real estate. Where will they strike next? So far this decade China has spent an estimated $115 billion on foreign acquisitions. Now the nation is sitting on massive foreign exchange wealth ($2.1 trillion and counting), it is eager to find something (anything!) to invest in besides US Treasury debt. In 2008, China's investments abroad doubled from $25 billion to $50 billion. China has only begun. And it won't stop anytime soon.

Writing in 2011, the chief economist of Standard Chartered Bank, Gerard Lyons, pithily summed up the current Western sentiment towards China's international business expansion as follows: 'The three most important words in the past decade were not the "War on Terror" but "Made in China". On present trends, the three most important words of this decade will be "Owned by China"' (quoted in *Financial Times*, 6 September 2011). It is essential for peaceful international relations that the multiple Western fears concerning China's rise are analysed in a balanced, thorough fashion. This short book is devoted to a single topic, namely a close analysis of the view that China is 'buying the world'.

1

Who are We? Who are They?[7]

Most people work in small and medium-sized firms. However, the core of the business system in the high-income countries is the large corporation. Much of the activity in the rest of the economy is linked to giant firms at the core of the system. In the three decades of capitalist globalization, the global business system has changed profoundly. Capitalist globalization has unleashed a process of intense industrial concentration, not only among the 'systems integrator' firms but also in the surrounding value chain. Oligopolistic competition across wide swathes of the global business system has produced unprecedented technical progress. The

---

[7] In 1990 and 1991 Robert Reich, US Secretary of Labor from 1993 to 1997, wrote two seminal articles in the *Harvard Business Review*, entitled 'Who is us?' (1990) and 'Who is them?' (1991). They were written in response to the fact that, on the one hand, internationalization of operations had already changed the nature of corporations with their headquarters in the United States and, on the other hand, non-US companies, both Japanese and European, were rapidly increasing their presence there. The issue of the identity of the US-based corporation was a central theme in Samuel Huntington's last major work, *Who are We?* (Huntington, 2005).

11

world of capitalist globalization looks far more like that envisaged by Karl Marx in *Das Kapital*, with the 'law of concentration' of capital, than the world of Alfred Marshall's *Principles of Economics*, in which competition was likened to the 'trees in the forest', with a constant rise and fall of positions and no tree rising above the level of the forest canopy. The firms that are the core of the global business system have expanded their international operations in a fashion that far exceeds what took place in any previous era. The global firm is increasingly detached from the political economy of its 'home' country. This raises fundamental questions about the identity of the firm, the nature of national industrial policy, and international relations. The transformation in the nature of the firm in the era of globalization poses a challenge for governments and citizens in the high-income countries.

Capitalist globalization poses a profound challenge also for developing countries, with China at the forefront. Since the early 1980s, in the face of continual advice from international institutions, especially the World

Writing in early 2011, Pascal Lamy, director-general of the World Trade Organization, argued that the transformation in the nature of international trade meant that it no longer made sense to think in terms of 'us' and 'them': 'International trade is currently measured in what is known as gross value. The total commercial value of an import is assigned to a single country of origin, as the good reaches customs. This worked fine when economist David Ricardo was alive: 200 years ago Portugal was trading wine "made in Portugal" for English textiles "made in England". But today the concept of country of origin is obsolete. What we call "made in China" is indeed assembled in China, but its commercial value comes from those numerous countries that precede its assembly. It no longer makes sense to think of trade in terms of "them" and "us"' (*Financial Times*, 24 January 2011).

Bank, and from many domestic economists, as well as intense pressure from giant global firms, the Chinese government has refused to privatize the commanding heights of its economy. Instead, China has attempted to build a team of giant globally competitive firms to match those of the high-income countries. Large Chinese firms, supported by national industrial policy, have made immense strides to reform their institutional structure and achieve technical progress. However, they remain mainly bound within their domestic economy. For several years the Chinese government has promoted the 'going out' policy for its national champions. The goal is to build global business systems that can compete in international markets with the world's leading multinationals.

Scarred by the experience of the Asian financial crisis of 1997, in the subsequent decade most Asian countries pursued policies that allowed them to accumulate large foreign exchange reserves. In 2011, China's foreign exchange reserves reached over $3.2 trillion, the largest of any country. There is a wide perception that China's giant companies can use these funds simply to 'buy the world', including our countries and companies. This is a serious misunderstanding of the nature of global competition. Giant global firms and the leading firms in their value chains are deeply embedded in the economic structure of both high-income and developing countries. They are also deeply embedded within China's own economy, occupying important segments of the domestic market. At the same time that large Chinese firms are beginning their attempt to 'go out' and build global business systems, leading global companies are accelerating their efforts to 'go in' to China.

Fear is often stimulated by lack of knowledge. In the midst of the dangerous situation in the global economy, the tense climate in international relations between China and the West, and the passionate outpouring of views in the global mass media, it is important that citizens in the high-income countries are presented with a balanced view of their own business system, that of China, and the place of each of them in the overall global political economy. In order to contribute to this urgent task, this book is organized around an enquiry into who 'we' are in the high-income countries and who 'they' are in the developing countries, with China as the focal point of the analysis. The relationship between 'us' in the high-income countries and 'them' in China cannot be usefully encapsulated by the phrase 'China buys the world'. To interpret the world in this fashion is profoundly misleading and damaging to peaceful international relations.

2

Who are We?

2.1 Globalization and industrial concentration[8]

After the 1970s the world economy entered a new phase of capitalist globalization. This involved revolutionary changes in information technology, widespread privatization, liberalization of international trade and investment flows, opening up of the former communist 'planned' economies, and comprehensive policy change in the formerly 'inward-looking' non-communist developing countries. The liberalization promoted across the world by the policies of the Washington Consensus[9]

[8] For an extended discussion of the issues in this section, see Nolan, 2001a, 2001b; Nolan, Zhang and Liu, 2007, 2008.

[9] The term 'Washington Consensus' refers to the policies advocated by the Washington-based international institutions, notably the International Monetary Fund and the World Bank, which formed the foundation for global economic liberalization after the 1970s. Since the time that these institutions were established in 1944 at the Bretton Woods Conference, they have been controlled firmly by the high-income countries. The head of the IMF has always been European, mostly a French person, and the head of the World Bank has always been an American. From the 1970s onwards the Washington Consensus institutions became increasingly

15

led to profound changes in the nature of the large corporation. Large firms with their headquarters in the high-income countries built global production systems, through both organic growth and explosive merger and acquisition. Their suppliers, also typically with their headquarters in the high-income countries, frequently followed them by themselves building global production systems. This period witnessed explosive industrial concentration among both giant 'system's integrator' firms and their supply chains.

Systems integrator firms

The period of the global business revolution witnessed massive asset restructuring, with firms extensively selling off 'non-core businesses' in order to develop their 'core businesses' and upgrade their asset portfolios. The goal for most large firms became the maintenance or establishment of their position as one of the handful of top companies in the global market-place. An unprecedented degree of industrial concentration was established among leading firms in sector after sector. By the 1980s, there was already a high degree of indus-

---

involved in formulating policy advice to developing countries and 'transition' economies. The policies included free trade, free international capital movements, a freely floating exchange rate, and privatization of state-owned enterprises. The ideology underlying the Washington Consensus is a belief that the free market based on private property rights is not only the most rational and efficient way to organize economic activity but also ethically superior to other approaches, since it provides maximum individual freedom of choice. The Washington Consensus approach to reform in the centrally planned economies is to divide policy-makers into 'reformers', who are considered to be 'good' because they favour 'free markets and freedom', and 'hardliners', who are considered to be 'bad' because they favour 'state control and corruption'.

trial concentration within many sectors of the individual high-income countries. However, the global business revolution saw for the first time the emergence of widespread industrial concentration across all high-income countries, as well as extending deeply into large parts of the developing world.

During the three decades of capitalist globalization, industrial concentration occurred in almost every sector. Alongside a huge increase in global output, the number of leading firms in most industrial sectors shrank and the degree of global industrial concentration increased greatly. The most visible part consists of the well-known firms with superior technologies and powerful brands. These constitute the 'systems integrators' or 'organizing brains' at the apex of extended value chains. Their main customers are the global middle class. By the early 2000s, within the high value-added, high-technology and strongly branded segments of global markets, which serve mainly the middle- and upper-income earners who control the bulk of the world's purchasing power, a veritable 'law' had come into play: a handful of giant firms, the 'systems integrators', occupied upwards of 50 per cent of the whole global market (see table 1).

The cascade effect

As they consolidated their leading positions, the systems integrator firms, with enormous procurement expenditure, exerted intense pressure upon the supply chain in order to minimize costs and stimulate technical progress. As firms struggled to meet the strict requirements that are the condition of their participation in the systems integrators' supply chains, industrial concentration

Table 1 Industrial concentration among systems integrator firms, 2006–9

Industrial sector	Number of firms	Global market share
Large commercial aircraft	2	100
20–90 seat commercial aircraft	2	75
Automobiles	10	77
Heavy-duty trucks	4	89[a]
Heavy- and medium-duty trucks	5	100[b]
Fixed-line telecoms infrastructure	5	83
Mobile telecoms infrastructure	3	77
PCs	4	55
Mobile handsets	3	65
Smartphones	3	75
Plasma TVs	5	80
LCD TVs	5	56
Digital cameras	6	80
Pharmaceuticals	10	69
Construction equipment	4	44
Agricultural equipment	3	69
Elevators	4	65
Soft drinks	5	>50
Carbonated soft drinks	2	70
Beer	4	59
Cigarettes	4	75[c]
Athletic footwear	2	55

[a] NAFTA only.
[b] Europe only.
[c] Excluding China.
All estimates of global market share are rough approximations only.
Source: *Financial Times*, various issues; company annual reports.

increased rapidly. In sector after sector, a small number of firms account for a major share of the market within each segment of the supply chain (see table 2).

This 'cascade effect' has profound implications for the nature of competition and technical progress. It means

Table 2 Industrial consolidation among selected firms within global value chains, 2006–8

Industrial sector	Number of firms	Combined global market share
Large commercial aircraft		
Engines	3[a]	100
Braking systems	2	75
Tyres	3	100
Seats	2	>50
Lavatory systems	1	>50
Wiring systems	1	>40
Titanium lockbolts	1	>50
Windows	1	>50
Automobiles		
Glass	3	75
Constant velocity joints	3	75
Tyres	3	55
Seats	2	>50
Braking systems	2	>50
Automotive steel	5	55
Information technology		
Micro-processors for PCs	2	100
Integrated circuits for wireless telecommunication	10	65
Database software	3	87
Enterprise resource planning programmes (ERP)	2	68
PC operating systems	1	90
DRAMS	5	82
Silicon wafers	4	89
Glass for LCD screens	2	78
Servers	2	63
Equipment to manufacture semiconductors	1	65
Beverages		
Cans	3	57
Glass containers	2	68

Table 2 *(continued)*

Industrial sector	Number of firms	Combined global market share
Industrial gases	3	80
High-speed bottling lines	2	85
Fork-lift trucks	2	50
PET bottle blowing equipment	1	75
Miscellaneous		
Cash-dispensing machines	2	72
Thermostats on electric kettles	1	66
Specialist steel plate	5	62
Aluminium	10	57
Goal gasification technology	3	89
Media and marketing advertising revenue	4	55
Search engine advertising revenue	1	70
Financial information publishing	2	77
Container shipping	10	58
Sheet glass	4	65

[a] Including GE's joint venture with Snecma.
All estimates of global market share are rough approximations only.
Source: *Financial Times*, various issues; company annual reports.

that the challenge confronting new entrant firms is far deeper than appears to be the case at first sight. Not only do they face immense difficulties in catching up with the leading systems integrators, who constitute the visible part of the 'iceberg' of industrial structure, they also face great difficulties in catching up with the powerful firms that now occupy the commanding heights in almost every segment of global supply chains, in the invisible part of the 'iceberg' that lies hidden from view beneath the water. Firms from developing countries are joining the 'global level playing field' at a point at which the concentration of business power has never been greater. In developing countries that liberalized their business systems in line with the Washington Consensus policies, oligopolies were established not only by the world's leading systems integrators but also in the upper reaches of the supply chain. Few people can imagine that just two firms produce 75 per cent of the global supply of braking systems for large commercial aircraft, that three firms produce 75 per cent of the global supply of constant velocity joints for automobiles, or that three firms produce 80 per cent of the global supply of industrial gases (table 2).

Planning and coordination: the external firm
If we define the firm not by the entity which is the legal owner but, rather, by the sphere over which conscious coordination of resource allocation takes place, then, far from becoming 'hollowed out' and much smaller in scope, the large firm can be seen to have enormously increased in size during the global business revolution. Alongside the disintegration of the large firm, the extent of conscious coordination over the surrounding value chain increased. In a wide range of business activities the organization of the value chain has developed into a comprehensively planned and coordinated activity. At its center is the core systems integrator. This firm typically possesses some combination of a number of key attributes, among them the capability to raise finance for large new projects and the resources necessary to fund a high level of R&D spending to sustain technological leadership, to develop a global brand, to invest in state-of-the-art information technology and to attract the

21

best human resources. Across a wide range of business types, from aircraft manufacture to fast-moving consumer goods, the core systems integrator interacts in the deepest, most intimate fashion with the major segments of the value chain, both upstream and downstream. This constitutes a new form of 'separation of ownership and control', in which the boundaries of the firm have become blurred. The numbers employed in the 'external firm' that is coordinated by the core firm, which possesses leading technologies and brands, typically far exceed the numbers employed in the core systems integrator firm.

Technical progress

In its 2007 survey, the UK Government's Department of Trade and Industry[10] compiled a survey of the R&D spending of the top 1,250 companies globally (the 'global 1,250') (DTI, 2007). In 2006, these firms invested around $430 billion in R&D. The list is 'strongly concentrated by company, sector and country'. The global 1,250 revealed a picture in which global technical progress in each sector is dominated by a small number of powerful firms. In 2008, the analysis was extended to cover the world's top 1,400 firms (the G1,400), which invested a total of $545 billion in R&D (BERR, 2008). This constitutes the main body of global investment in technical progress. The top 100 firms account for 60 per

---

[10] After 2007 the DTI was successively renamed the Department for Business Enterprise and Regulatory Reform (BERR) and the Department of Business, Innovation and Skills (BIS). In 2008 the number of companies in the survey increased to 1,400, but in 2009 the number was reduced to 1,000, and in 2010 the decision was made for budgetary reasons to cease publication of this invaluable piece of research.

cent of the total R&D spending of the G1,400, while the bottom 100 firms account for less than 1 per cent of the total. In other words, around 100 or so firms in a small number of high-technology industries sit at the centre of technical progress in the era of globalization. Within each sector there was a high degree of industrial concentration of R&D expenditure (see table 3). Within the G1,400, the top ten firms accounted for 46 per cent of investment in the technology hardware and equipment sector, 61 per cent in health-care equipment and services, 65 per cent in autos and components, 65 per cent in chemicals, 68 per cent in software and computer services, and 80 per cent in aerospace.

Far from witnessing a reduction in the level of competition, the recent period has seen a drastic increase in the intensity of competition, and investment in technical progress is a key source of competitive advantage. The DTI study concluded: 'Large companies are pouring money into research and development at an unprecedented rate, in response to growing competition ... In many sectors profits are growing strongly and companies can afford to spend more on R&D ... Where profits are weak, such as in the automobile industry, the competition is so fierce that companies dare not cut their investment' (DTI, 2007). Between 2001–2 and 2005–6, total R&D expenditure by the top 1,250 companies rose by 23 per cent (ibid.), and between 2005–6 and 2009–10 total spending by the top 1,000 companies increased by a further 30 per cent (BIS, 2010). In other words, between 2001–2 and 2009–10, R&D spending by the world's top 1,000 or so companies increased by around three-fifths.

Table 3 Industrial concentration and the global business revolution: global 1,400 R&D investment, 2007

Sector	Share of total G1,400 R&D investment (%)	Number of firms	Share of sectoral investment in R&D (%)	
			Top five firms	Top ten firms
Aerospace and military	4.1	41	62	80
Autos and auto components	16.9	84	41	65
Chemicals	4.4	95	39	56
Electronics and electrical equipment	7.0	117	48	61
Health-care equipment and services	1.8	59	42	57
Pharmaceuticals and biotechnology	19.1	178	35	57
Software and computer services	7.1	122	54	68
Technology hardware and equipment	18.3	224	28	46
Others	21.3	480	–	–
Total	100.0	1,400		

Source: BERR, 2008.

24

2.2 Evidence from automobiles and beverages

The automobile industry and the beverage industry have fundamentally different characteristics. Automobiles are at the forefront of technical progress, with continuous change in the nature of the product. They cost thousands of dollars per item and last for many years. Beverages incorporate minimal technical progress with small amounts of product innovation. In most cases they cost small amounts per item and are consumed instantly.[11] However, despite their fundamental differences, these two strikingly different sectors have exhibited remarkably similar trends in terms of industrial consolidation during the era of capitalist globalization.

Automobiles

The global stock of automobiles grew from 150 million in 1950 to 800 million in 2000, and is predicted to rise to around 1,600 million in 2030. In 1960 there were forty-two independent automobile assemblers in North America, Western Europe and Japan. Through an intensive process of merger and acquisition that number has now shrunk to just fifteen firms. Among these are five giant auto assemblers, with revenues in 2010 ranging from $108 billion to $221 billion, that account for over one-half of global passenger vehicle output. The top ten auto assemblers, which are all from high-income countries, account for almost 80 per cent of total global output. Even the leading automobile firms face threats to their survival due to the intense oligopolistic

---

[11] Expensive wines are an exception.

competition. It is difficult for an auto assembler to survive with an output of fewer than around 5 million vehicles per year.[12]

In order to survive in this ferocious competition, the leading assemblers must spend large amounts on R&D, in order to make vehicles lighter in weight, reduce CO_2 emissions, and improve fuel efficiency, safety, durability and reliability. The world's top auto assembler, Toyota, spends almost $10 billion on R&D, and the top five firms each spend over $6 billion (BIS, 2009). They also each spend several billion dollars each year on building their global brands.

The leading auto assemblers each spend several tens of billions of dollars annually on procurement of materials and components. GM, for example, has an annual procurement spend of around US$80 billion. As the leading automobile assemblers have grown in terms of the scope and size of their markets since the 1970s, so also has the intensity of pressure they have imposed upon their supply chains. The pressure upon suppliers is felt most visibly in terms of price. However, the relationship is far from arm's-length. The assemblers have selected a group of powerful sub-system integrator firms that are able to partner them in their global expansion: 'We're looking for the top suppliers to help us grow in the market place. As we grow, they will grow with us' (GM website). The leading auto assemblers work together to plan the

---

[12] The main exception is the luxury vehicle sector. In 2009 the top two luxury vehicle assemblers, Mercedes and BMW, produced only 1.7 million and 1.2 million passenger vehicles, respectively. However, within the luxury vehicle sector they have a global market share of around 70 per cent.

supplier firm's investment in new production locations close to the assemblers. Leading components suppliers, such as Bosch, Delphi, Valeo, Denso, Johnson Controls, ZF, Bridgestone and Michelin, each have more than 100 production plants across the world, close at hand to the assembly plants in order to minimize transport costs and inventories through 'just-in-time' supply.

There is a deep interaction between the direction of the core strategic suppliers' R&D and the needs of the assemblers. The leading auto assemblers have put intense pressure on leading components suppliers to invest large amounts in R&D to meet the the formers' needs. In 2010 the leading components supplier, Robert Bosch, spent $5.1 billion on R&D, and the seven leading components suppliers – all from the high-income countries – each spent around $1 billion or more (BIS, 2010).

The key suppliers themselves spend large amounts on their own procurement. Robert Bosch spends over $25 billion annually on purchasing inputs. Sub-system integrators are deepening their relationship with their own suppliers beyond a simple price relationship. For example, Delphi is developing a group of its own seventy to eighty key 'strategic suppliers': 'These are the suppliers we'd like to grow with, they understand our cost models, where we are going, and being increasingly willing to put more of their research and development and engineering money behind projects for us.'

Due to the intense pressure from the cascade effect, the auto components industry has been through a dramatic transition since the 1970s. The enormous rise in car volumes at the top assemblers has triggered a 'Darwinian struggle for survival' among the components suppliers, the number of which expanded from an estimated 20,000 in 1950 to over 40,000 in 1970. However, by 1990 the number had fallen to under 30,000. During the epoch of revolutionary growth and consolidation of the vehicle assemblers, the number of components makers shrank to fewer than 5,000 in 2000 and is predicted to fall still further, to fewer than 3,000 by 2015.

A handful of components makers have emerged, mainly through merger and acquisition, to dominate the upper reaches of the auto components supply chain. In each segment of the vehicle, a small number of sub-systems integrators, each with their own supply chains, dominate the global market. For example, four firms (Continental, Denso, Nippon Seiki and JCI) account for 57 per cent of global auto instrumentation displays; just three firms account for 55 per cent of total world production of auto tyres (Michelin, Bridgestone and Goodyear), 75 per cent of the world output of auto glass (Asahi, St Gobain and NSG) and 75 per cent of the global market for constant velocity joints (GKN, NTN and Delphi); while just two firms account for around three-quarters of the world's production of diesel fuel injection pumps (Bosch and Delphi), over one-half of all the automobile seat systems supplied to assemblers in Europe and North America (Johnson Controls and Lear), around 50 per cent of the global total of anti-locking brake systems and electronic stability control systems (Bosch and Continental) and 57 per cent of telematics equipment (Continental and LG). In each segment of the vehicle there is intense oligopolistic competition among the sub-systems integrators.

Beverages

Since the 1980s, the global beverage industry has witnessed high-speed consolidation. Consolidation has been driven by the enormous economies of scale in this industry, including procurement spending, systems integration skills across the whole supply chain, and spending on media and marketing, as well as the pressure arising from the consolidation of global customers in retail (e.g., WalMart, Carrefour, Metro, Ahold and Tesco), quick-service restaurants (e.g., McDonald's, Pizza Hut and KFC)[13] and entertainment chains (e.g., Disney).

In the carbonated soft drinks sector, just two firms now account for around three-quarters of total global sales. In the broader category of non-alcoholic drinks, just five firms account for over one-half of the global market. The beer industry has also experienced high-speed industrial consolidation. Four companies have emerged from this process at the apex of the global industry. Between them Anheuser-Busch Inbev (ABI), SAB Miller-Molson Coors, Heineken and Carlsberg, all with their headquarters in the high-income countries, occupy around three-fifths of the total global market for beer. Their main customers are the global middle class. The fact that the beverage industry is dominated globally by a handful of giant firms is not inconsistent with the existence of a huge number of small firms, employing large numbers of people in the 'informal sector', that make mainly low-quality products for poor people. In addition there are numerous small firms that

---

[13] Both KFC and Pizza Hut are subsidiaries of Yum! Brands.

manufacture specialist products for a small niche of people with high incomes.[14]

ABI is at the forefront of consolidation in the beer industry. It was the product of Inbev's $52 billion acquisition in 2008 of the North American giant brewer Anheuser-Busch. However, Inbev was itself the culmination of a long process of merger and acquisition, which included the merger in 1987 of Belgium's two largest brewers, Artois and Piedboeuf, to form Interbrew and the merger in 1999 of Brazil's two giant brewers Antarctica and Brama to form Ambev. Both Ambev and Interbrew embarked separately on numerous international acquisitions before they merged to form Inbev in 2004. In 2010 ABI had fourteen brands each with sales revenues of more than $1 billion, among them the global brands Stella Artois, Budweiser and Beck's. It produced 34 per cent of its beer volume in North America, 36 per cent in Latin America, 15 per cent in Europe and 12 per cent in Asia-Pacific. Its products occupied the first or second position in the beer market in nineteen countries, including a market share of 48 per cent in the United States and 70 per cent in Brazil. In 2010 its revenues reached $34 billion with profits of $5.8 billion.

The leading beverage companies have large expenditure on the procurement of inputs. For example, the

---

[14] The explosive concentration of the global beer industry is not inconsistent with the mushrooming of myriads of 'micro-breweries' producing 'real ale'. The English county of Yorkshire contains more than seventy micro-breweries. However, their total market share is extremely small and they do not offer meaningful competition to the huge volumes sold by the global brewers.

Coca-Cola business system (covering both the Coca-Cola Company and its bottlers) spends over $50 billion annually on procurement. The massive expenditure on material inputs and services by the world's leading beverage producers has increased the pressure for consolidation within the higher reaches of the supply chain. There is intense pressure to lower costs and prices. There is intense pressure to achieve technical progress in order to make packaging lighter, to improve its appearance, and to make it safer and more recyclable, easier to handle, and better able to keep the product in good condition. There is intense pressure also to establish networks of global plants close to the bottling plants in order to minimize transport and inventory costs through 'just-in-time' supply.

The 'cascade effect' has stimulated a wave of consolidation in the beverage industry's supply chain. Global beverage companies frequently intervene in the supply chain to encourage transformation of the institutional structure in order to meet their requirements. Moreover, as the higher reaches of the supply chain have struggled to meet the global needs of the world's leading companies, the process of consolidation within their ranks has produced further 'cascade' pressure on the supply chain of these firms, as they struggle to lower costs and achieve the technical progress necessary to meet the fierce demands of the world's leading system integrators who stand at the centre of their respective supply chains.

Global consumer packaging is a huge industry, worth about $300 billion annually. The top ten global packaging firms account for between 40 and 80 per cent of global markets, depending on the sector. The world's leading beverage firms interact closely with the leaders of the packaging industry, working together to meet their specific needs through innovations in product and process technologies. Key pressures on the packaging industry have included cost and weight reduction, improved customer safety, increased product life and enhanced appearance. Technical progress has also been achieved through contributions from the primary material suppliers in the aluminium, steel and PET resin industries, as well as in the suppliers of machinery. The world's leading beverage firms have interacted with this process at every step, acting as 'systems integrators' for the overall process of technical progress, and nurturing institutional change so that leading suppliers have sufficient scale to meet their strict requirements. Although the beverage industry is a 'low-technology' industry with a low level of spending on R&D, many parts of the supply chain use high technologies and require high levels of spending on R&D in order to meet the intense demands from the beverage companies.

Over 200 billion beverage cans are consumed annually. Since the late 1980s, the world's metal can industry has rapidly consolidated. Three firms now stand out as the global industry leaders, with a combined market share of 57 per cent. In 2007, the world's leading can maker, Rexam, produced around 58 billion metal cans, of which it sold around 24 billion to Coca-Cola. Glass bottles are still the main form of primary packaging in the beer industry, and, despite their relative decline, remain an important form of packaging for soft drinks, especially in developing countries. Following successive rounds of merger and acquisition in the 1990s, the glass bottle industry has become highly consolidated. The two super-giants of the industry (Owens-Illinois and Saint-Gobain) now account for around 68 per cent of total production in Europe and North America. Between them they produce more than 60 billion glass bottles annually.

PET (plastic) bottles were developed in the late 1960s, and quickly became the most important form of primary packaging in the soft drinks industry. In recent years the industry has become increasingly concentrated. Much of the technical progress in the PET bottle industry has been achieved by the specialist machine builders, who make two different types of machinery, including equipment to manufacture 'pre-forms' and equipment that 'blows' the pre-forms into their final bottle form. Each of these sectors is dominated by specialist high-technology firms. One firm alone (Husky) accounts for around three-quarters of the total global market for high-volume PET injection machines to manufacture pre-forms, while another specialist firm, Tetra Laval, through its Sidel subsidiary, has a near monopoly on the purchase of advanced blowing equipment by the world's leading beverage companies.

Following intense mergers and acquisitions, the industrial gas sector now has just three firms that dominate the industry. The M&A frenzy concluded with the acquisition of the UK-based company BOC ('British Oxygen Company') by the German-based industrial gas giant Linde, which now has around 29 per cent of the global market. Its two main competitors, Air Liquide (French-based) and Praxair (US-based), have around 41 per cent of the global market, so that the three firms together have around 70 per cent of the entire global market.

In the supply of beverage-filling line equipment, the high value-added, high-technology segments of the market supplying the world's leading beverage companies are dominated by just two firms (KHS and Krones), the product of ceaseless M&A, which together account for almost nine-tenths of global sales of high-speed beverage bottling lines. The world's leading beverage companies buy machines almost exclusively from these two companies because of their high levels of reliability, low operating costs, high speed, consistent filling height, and low rates of damage to bottles and product. Each of them spends heavily on research and development.

The world's leading beverage companies are among the largest purchasers of trucks. Their fleets are enormous, amounting to hundreds of thousands of trucks for the industry leaders. For example, the Coca-Cola system has a total of over 500,000 trucks that it either owns itself or are operated by 'third party' trucking companies. The world's leading truck manufacturers experience intense pressure from their global customers to lower costs and improve technologies. This intensifies the pressure to increase scale in order to achieve greater volume of procurement and push down costs across their own value chains, including suppliers of truck components (engines, brake systems, tyres, exhaust systems, seats, informatics and ventilation systems) and materials (steel, aluminium and plastics). Greater scale also enables them to achieve faster technical progress through economies of scope (coordinated technical progress that can be used in different divisions of the company) in order to provide the customer with more reliability, lower fuel costs, greater safety and more effective ability to meet pollution control requirements.

Since the 1980s, industrial concentration in the truck industry has greatly increased. The industry has a remarkably successful record of international M&A. These include German-based Mercedes' acquisition of Freightliner, Ford Heavy Trucks division and Western Star (all in North America); US-based Paccar's acquisition of Foden and Leyland (both UK companies) and DAF (Netherlands); and Swedish-based Volvo's acquisition of Renault Trucks (France), Mack (USA) and Nissan Diesel (Japan). Moreover, German-based VW recently acquired majority ownership of Scania (Sweden) and a controlling equity share in MAN, so that they essentially form a single giant truck company.[15] In Europe, five truck makers (Mercedes, Volvo, VW/ MAN/Scania, Paccar and Iveco) produce 100 per cent of the trucks. In the US the top four companies (Mercedes, Paccar, Volvo and Navistar) account for nine-tenths of the market for heavy-duty trucks. The world's top five truck makers account for one-half of total global sales in terms of the number of units sold but a much higher share of the total market value, as the leading companies produce far higher technology vehicles with much higher prices than those produced by manufacturers in developing countries.

---

[15] In September 2011 the European competition authorities approved VW's offer to acquire full control of MAN. The decision by the authorities was triggered by VW's increase in its equity ownership share in MAN to 30 per cent, which required it to make an offer for full control.

Common elements in the supply chain of automobiles and beverages

In both the auto and the beverage industries there is intense pressure on leading suppliers to establish a network of plants across the world, close to the systems integrators. Typically, a large fraction of these 'clusters of small and medium-sized plants' are not independent firms but, rather, the local subsidiaries of large global companies.

The auto industry is one of the biggest users of steel and aluminium. Pressure from the cascade effect has been a major stimulus for the consolidation in the steel industry and, to a lesser extent, the aluminium industry. The metal can industry is also a significant consumer of both aluminium and steel and places intense pressure on these industries to achieve technical progress, improve product quality and lower costs. The other major users of primary metals have also consolidated at high speed during the global business revolution, among them the automobile, construction, household durable goods and aerospace industries. In turn they place intense pressure on the metallurgical industries, which have experienced rapid consolidation. The top five firms produce over two-fifths of world production of aluminium and an even higher share of the aluminium sheet for beverage cans. In the steel industry, leading steel firms focus on high value-added, high-technology products for global customers, including steel for beverage cans. ArcelorMittal alone accounts for an estimated 26 per cent of the total global production of automotive steel, and the top five firms (ArcelorMittal, Nippon Steel, JFE, US Steel and ThyssenKrupp) account for over one-half of global auto steel production.

Branding is crucial for both auto and beverage companies, who are key customers of the media and marketing industry. Auto and beverage firms together account for a large share of the revenues of the leading firms in the sector. The media and marketing industry has witnessed intense M&A activity alongside the global expansion of their main customers. The world's top ten companies each spend an average of $2 to $3 billion annually on different aspects of branding. The media and marketing industry has polarized into a small number of immensely powerful firms and a large number of small firms. The top four firms in the sector (WPP, Omnicom, Interpublic and Publicis) account for around three-fifths of global advertising revenue. Each of them has grown through intense merger and acquisition, with numerous subsidiaries, each of which retains its own identity but benefits from economies of scale at the level of the whole company.

Accounting and related services are crucial for a global firm in any sector. Without reliable, independent audits, financial markets cannot reach a judgement about their investments. The accounting profession has low barriers to entry, and across the world there are many thousands of small firms in this sector. However, the industry has become highly concentrated in terms of accounting services for global firms. Before 1987 there were just eight giant accountancy firms that dominated the industry, but today there are only four (Ernst and Young, PwC, KPMG and Deloitte Touche Tohmatsu). Among the firms in the FTSE 100, all but one is audited by the Big Four and, among the FTSE 250, 240 firms are audited by the Big Four.

Table 4 Relative growth of trade and FDI, 1990–2009

	1990	2009
FDI inward stock ($ billion)	2,082	17,743
FDI outward stock ($ billion)	2,087	18,982
Total assets of foreign affiliates ($ billion)	5,938	77,057
Sales of foreign affiliates ($ billion)	6,026	29,298
Exports of foreign affiliates ($ billion)	1,498	5,186
Employment by foreign affiliates (million)	24.5	79.8
World GDP ($ billion, current prices)	22,121	55,005
World exports of goods and services ($ billion)	4,414	15,716
World exports/world GDP (%)	20.0	28.6
Sales of foreign affiliates/world GDP (%)	27.2	53.2
Sales of foreign affiliates/world exports (%)	137	186
Exports of foreign affiliates/world exports (%)	33.9	33.0
Assets of foreign affiliates/world GDP (%)	26.7	140.0
Inward FDI/world GDP (%)	9.4	32.3

Source: UNCTAD, 2010: 16.

2.3 Globalization and 'going out' by global firms

Building global business systems

Liberalization of trade flows has been a centrally important part of globalization. In the past two decades, world exports quadrupled in value and the share of world exports in global GDP rose from 20 per cent to 29 per cent (see table 4). However, the growth of international investment by transnational firms proceeded at a much faster pace than the growth of world trade. In 1990 the sales of foreign affiliates were equivalent to 27 per cent of world GDP. By 2009 this had risen to 53 per cent and the sales of foreign affiliates were almost double world exports. After three decades of globalization and 'going out', the international assets, sales and employment of giant companies have outgrown those of the economy where they are headquartered. The foreign assets of the world's 100 largest multinational companies are 57 per cent of their total assets, foreign employment amounts to 58 per cent of total employment, and foreign sales amount to 61 per cent of total sales (UNCTAD, 2010).

Intertwining of the business systems of high-income countries: 'I have you within me and you have me within you'

During the era of capitalist globalization the business structures of developed countries became increasingly intertwined. Firms with their headquarters in one developed country 'went out' into other developed countries at the same time that firms from other developed countries 'came in' to the home country. Between 1990 and 2009, the stock of outward FDI from the developed countries increased more than eightfold, rising from 11 per cent to 41 per cent of GDP. Most of this increase was in other developed countries. At the same time, the stock of inward FDI in the developed countries rose sevenfold, from 9 per cent to 32 per cent of GDP. By 2009, the inward stock of FDI amounted to 22 per cent of GDP in the United States, 21 per cent in Germany, 43 per cent in France, and 52 per cent in the UK (see table 5).

Among the high-income countries, the UK has been one of the most liberal in permitting inward investment since the 1970s. It seems as if a 'for sale' sign has been hung outside the UK's corporate sector. The inward stock of FDI increased from 11.7 per cent of GDP in 1980 to 51.7 per cent in 2009. A long list of iconic UK non-financial companies was acquired by firms from other

Table 5 Increase in FDI during globalization

| | Inward FDI stock | | | | Increase, 1990–2009 ($ billion) (%) |
| | 1990 | | 2009 | | |
	$ billion	% GDP	$ billion	% GDP	
Developed countries	1,557	9.0	12,352	31.5	10,795 (69)
of which: USA	540	9.3	3,121	21.9	2,581 (16)
UK	204	20.6	1,125	51.7	921 (6)
France	98	7.9	1,133	42.8	1,035 (7)
Germany	111	6.5	701	21.0	590 (4)
Japan	10	0.3	200	3.9	190 (1)
Developing countries	525	13.6	4,893	29.1	4,368 (28)
SE Europe and CIS[a]	negl.	0.4	497	27.5	497 (3)
World	2,081	9.8	17,743	30.7	15,662 (100)

Outward FDI stock

	1990		2009		
	$ billion	% GDP	$ billion	% GDP	
Developed countries	1,942	11.2	16,011	40.8	14,069 (84)
of which: USA	732	12.6	4,303	30.2	3,571 (21)
UK	229	23.1	1,652	76.0	1,423 (8)
France	112	9.0	1,720	64.9	1,608 (10)
Germany	152	8.8	1,378	41.2	1,226 (7)
Japan	201	6.7	741	14.6	540 (3)
Developing countries	145	4.1	2,691	16.5	2,546 (15)
SE Europe and CIS[a]	0		280	16.1	280 (1)
World	2,087	10.0	18,982	33.2	16,805 (100)

[a] South-Eastern Europe and the Commonwealth of Independent States.
UNCTAD includes as 'developing economies' not only Taiwan, but also countries such as Singapore, Hong Kong, Kuwait, Qatar and the Republic of Korea, which the World Bank classifies as 'high-income countries'.

high-income countries, among them Allied Domecq, Autonomy, BOC, BAA, British Paper Board, British Energy, Cadbury, Foden Trucks, Hanson, ICI, Jaguar and Land Rover,[16] Leyland Trucks, Marconi, O2, Perkins Engine Company, Pilkington, Rolls-Royce Motor Cars, Scottish & Newcastle, Scottish Power, Smiths Aerospace and Wellstream. In the financial sector, Abbey National, Barings, Cazenove, Flemings, Kleinwort, Midland Bank, Morgan Grenfell and Schroders were all acquired by firms from other high-income countries. The UK subsidiaries of many global companies, including their new acquisitions, have multi-billion dollar sales revenue from their operations in the UK. These often dwarf the UK sales of UK firms in the same sectors and frequently have substantial R&D investments in the UK and several thousand UK employees. It seems to many people that there is little left of 'UK plc'.

However, this view is deeply misleading. At the same time that large swathes of the 'commanding heights' of UK business were sold to firms from other high-income countries, British companies accelerated their international expansion both through organic growth and, especially, through intense merger and acquisition activity. Moreover, a succession of powerful international firms moved their headquarters to the UK and 'acquired British passports', including HSBC (from Hong Kong), Anglo-American, Old Mutual and SABMiller (all from South Africa). Firms with their headquarters in the UK are at the forefront of the globalization of business. The

---

[16] After their sale to Ford, these iconic, but loss-making, car companies were subsequently sold to Tata Automotive, from India.

UK's outward stock of FDI increased from 15.0 per cent of GDP in 1980 to 76.0 per cent in 2009, far above the average for the developed countries as a whole.

After three decades of capitalist globalization the UK has a group of companies that are at the forefront of their respective industrial sectors, including aerospace, oil, mining, telecommunications services, retail, banking, insurance, pharmaceuticals, media and marketing, tobacco and alcoholic drinks. In 2009 the UK had thirty-two companies in the FT 500, compared with twenty-three for France and twenty for Germany. These companies had the third largest total market capitalization of any country in the FT 500. The UK's stock of outward FDI stood at $1,652 billion, second only to the USA (see table 5). Its stock of inward investment stood at $1,125 billion, only two-thirds of its outward FDI.

As the international operations of leading UK firms have expanded, so these have come to dwarf their domestic operations. The foreign assets, revenues and employment of most of the UK's leading companies now greatly exceed those in the domestic UK economy (see table 6). This is the case for giant UK-based companies such as BP, Shell, SABMiller, HSBC, Standard Chartered, Anglo-American, Unilever, AstraZeneca, Vodafone, BAE Systems, GKN, WPP, BAT and Imperial Tobacco. However, it is also the case for medium-sized firms that are global leaders in their particular segments of the global value chain, such as Meggitt and Cobham in aerospace components, IMI in fluid control components and beverage dispensers, and Rexam in the beverage can industry.

Table 6 International operations of selected UK companies, 2008

Company	Foreign assets		Foreign sales		Foreign employment	
	$ billion	% total	$ billion	% total	'000s	% total
Vodafone	205	91	52	87	69	87
Shell	222	79	261	57	85	83
BP	188	82	284	78	76	94
Anglo-American	44	88	22	85	95	90
Astra Zeneca	38	81	31	97	55	83
BAE Systems	33	89	20	83	61	65
WPP	32	91	10	91	88	91
Unilever	33	66	39	70	130	75
GSK	27	47	23	66	54	55
SABMiller	25	78	56	75	75	81
BAT	20	50	10	56	75	78
GKN	–	–	–	–	33	86
Cobham	1.7	83	2.7	91	9	79
Meggitt	2.7	77	1.44	88	5	73
Rexam	5.9	96	6.8	96	22	97
IMI	0.7	82	2.4	93	11	84

Source: UNCTAD, 2009; annual reports of various companies.

Germany stands at the forefront of international trade in high value-added goods. However, the relationship between Germany's leading firms and the international economy has also undergone profound change in recent years. Germany's leading firms in a wide array of sectors have greatly expanded their international operations, building production systems outside the country, so that their international operations greatly exceed their domestic operations (see table 7). The international assets, sales and employment of giant German firms such as VW, Siemens, BASF and

Who are We?

Table 7 International operations of selected German companies (foreign assets, sales and employment as a percentage of the total)

	Assets	*Sales*	*Employment*
E.on	64	42	61
VW	52	75	53
Siemens	77	72	69
Bosch	–	76	60
Continental	–	71	67
MAN	–	78	45
Deutsche Telekom	55	53	42
Allianz	–	74[a]	68
Daimler	48	77	38
BMW	45	79	26
RWE	42	38	41
BASF	61	56	51
Deutsche Post	–	66	63
ThyssenKrupp	52	64	57
Linde	91	94	85
Metro	62	61	61
Bayer	36	52	49
SAP	–	81	69
Infineon	–	63	82
Heidelberg Cement[b]	>70	92	>66
Adidas[c]	–	>80	>90
Merck	–	79	>44[d]

[a] Proportion of customers.
[b] More than 66 per cent of its employees and more than 70 per cent of Heidelberg's cement capacity are located outside Western and Northern Europe.
[c] Adidas sports shoes (Adidas, Reebok and Rockport brands) are produced entirely by 270 independent manufacturing partners, almost 70 per cent of them in China. Less than 10 per cent of the 39,000 direct employees work in the company's head office in Germany. If the numbers employed indirectly in the independent supplier companies are included, then the proportion of workers in Germany would shrink to a minuscule level.
[d] 44 per cent of Merck employees are outside Europe.
Source: UNCTAD, 2010; company annual reports.

ThyssenKrupp greatly exceed their domestic levels. The expansion of the international operations of such firms is typically accompanied by the internationalization of the operations of the leading firms within their respective supply chains, such as Bosch and Continental in auto sub-systems, Linde in industrial gases, SAP in software, and Infineon in semiconductors.

Even though the USA is a continental-sized economy, most of its leading companies now have over one-half of their assets, sales and employment outside the country (see table 8). In the 1970s, companies such as Coca-Cola still had the majority of their assets, sales and employment within the USA itself. In the era of capitalist globalization the main body of leading American firms have built international business systems. This applies not only to the leading systems integrator firms but also to firms that occupy key positions within the global supply chain, such as Alcoa (aluminium products), Schlumberger (oilfield services), United Technology (aircraft engines, high-speed lifts and air conditioning systems) and Praxair (industrial gases).

Between 1987 and 2008 there were 2,219 cross-border 'mega-mergers' of over $1 billion, with a total value of $7,232 billion (UNCTAD, 2009: 11). In other words, over 2,200 large firms 'gave up their national passport'. In most cases firms from one high-income country gave up their passport to firms from other high-income countries. It could be said of their business systems after three decades of globalization: 'You have me within you, and I have you within me.'

The relationship between giant multinational companies and their home countries has progressively

Table 8 International operations of selected US companies: foreign (non-US) assets, sales and employment as a proportion of the total (%), 2008

	Foreign assets	Foreign sales	Foreign employment
General Electric	50	53	53
ExxonMobil	71	70	63
Chevron	66	56	52
Ford	46	59	58
ConocoPhillips	55	31	45
Procter & Gamble	47	61	73
WalMart	38	25	31
IBM	47	65	71
Pfizer	44	58	61
General Motors	45	49	52
Johnson & Johnson	48	49	59
Liberty Global	100	100	59
Alcoa	71	47	66
United Technologies	47	52	65
Kraft Foods	41	49	60
Coca-Cola	62	75	86
Schlumberger	78	76	78
Caterpillar[a]	–	62[b]	53[b]
Praxair[c]	61	64	61
Dow[c]	52	67	49[b]

[a] 2009.
[b] Outside North America.
[c] 2010.
Source: UNCTAD, 2010; company annual reports.

weakened. Their identity and interests are bound up less and less with those of the country in which they happen to have their headquarters. Leading international firms have less and less incentive to cooperate with the national governments of the countries in which they have their headquarters in order to construct a 'national industrial policy'. In turn, these national governments have less and less incentive to support 'national champion' firms, since the latter have steadily reduced their relationship with the home country. Political parties and national governments in the high-income countries must respond to the widespread suspicion and jealousy, and even outright hostility, among ordinary citizens towards the privileged group who work in the giant global firms. Attacking 'big business' wins votes. Most people work for small companies producing goods and services for the domestic market rather than for global firms. For example, in the USA, small businesses, which are those that employ fewer than 500 workers, account for two-thirds of total employment and around one-half of national output. Ordinary citizens feel bewildered and threatened by the 'desertion' of their country by the global firm. The employees of global firms inhabit the world of business-class air travel, Blackberries, CNN, the Financial Times and a 'borderless world'. However, most of their friends and relatives, who constitute the main body of voters in the high-income countries, live in a quite different, 'non-global world'. For them, 'global' means at the most a package holiday in a foreign country.

Disparity in business power between firms from developed countries and firms from developing countries

The 'commanding heights' of the global business system are dominated by firms from high-income countries. The number of firms from low- and middle-income countries in the FT 500 has increased substantially in recent years. In 2010 there were seventy-nine, compared with just eight in the year 2000. However, this is still a small number in relation to the population of developing countries. Moreover, such firms are concentrated in a narrow range of sectors, including twenty-three banks, sixteen oil and gas producers, eleven metals and mining companies, and nine telecommunications service companies. Most of these operate in protected domestic markets and are often state-owned enterprises which cannot be acquired by multinational companies. Moreover, these are sectors that mainly make use of high technology but do not themselves generate new technology. In the FT 500 (2010) there were no firms at all from developing countries in aerospace, chemicals, electronic and electrical equipment, retail, gas, water and utilities, health care, pharmaceuticals, industrial engineering, media, oil equipment and services, personal goods, or information technology hardware, and just one in the automobile parts and components sector.

Firms from developing countries still lag far behind those from the high-income countries in terms of research and development. Firms from a small group of countries dominate the list of G1,400 companies (BERR, 2008). Firms from the USA, Japan, Germany, France and the UK account for 80 per cent of the total number. Five small European countries (Denmark, Finland, Sweden, Switzerland and the Netherlands), with a total population of 42 million people, have 132 firms in the G1,400, while the four 'BRIC' countries (Brazil, Russia, India and China), with a total population of 2.6 billion, have thirty-four firms in the G1,400. The low- and middle-income countries as a whole, which have 84 per cent of the world's population, have a total of just thirty-seven firms in the G1,400.

In 2009, after three decades of capitalist globalization, firms from developing countries were almost entirely absent from the list of the world's top 1,000 firms in terms of R&D spending (BIS, 2009):

- *Aerospace* The world's top thirty-four firms in the aerospace industry spent a total of $21 billion on R&D. Embraer, ranked seventeenth in the sector in terms of spending, is the only one of these from a developing country. Its spend in 2008–9 was $197 million, compared with $3.8 billion at both Boeing and EADS. Its revenue was $6.3 billion, compared with more than $60 billion each at Boeing and EADS.

- *Automobiles and components* The world's top seventy-three firms in the automobile and components industry spent a total of $99 billion on R&D. Only one firm, Tata Motors (India), was from a developing country, and its spend in 2008–9 was $303 million. Toyota Motors spent over $10 billion in 2008–9, and the top fourteen firms all spent more than $3 billion each.

- *Chemicals* The top seventy-seven firms in the world's chemical industry spent a total of $26 billion on R&D. Not one was from a developing country.

- *Electronics and electrical equipment* The world's top eighty-two firms in the electronics and electrical equipment sector spent a total of $45 billion on R&D. There was only one firm from a developing economy – BYD (China) – which spent $148 million in 2008–9, compared with over $5 billion each for Samsung and Siemens.[17]

- *Industrial engineering* The world's top sixty-five firms in the industrial engineering sector spent a total of $16.2 billion on R&D. There were just four firms from developing countries among them: China South Locomotive, Shanghai Electric and Dongfang Electric (all from China) and Bharat Heavy Electrical (India).

- *Pharmaceutical and biotechnology* The world's top 116 firms in the pharmaceutical and biotechnology sector spent a total of $108 billion on R&D. Not one was from a developing country.

- *Software and computer services* The world's top sixty-nine firms in software and computer services spent a total of $39.6 billion on R&D. There were just four firms from developing countries among them. These were Polaris Software, Mindtree and KPIT Cummins from India[18] and Tencent from China. The highest ranked of these was Polaris Software (India), with a spend of $154 million, compared with over $9 billon by Microsoft, the top-ranked firm in the sector.

- *Leisure goods* The world's top twenty-eight firms spent a total of $23 billion on R&D. Not one was from a developing country.

---

[17] There were eleven firms from Taiwan. However, Taiwan is a high-income economy, with an average per capita income of (PPP) $32,000, the same level as Spain.

[18] KPIT Cummins is a joint venture between KPIT and the global giant diesel engine manufacturer Cummins. Its main function is to produce software solutions for Cummins.

- *Technology hardware and equipment* The world's top 159 firms in this sector spent a total of $99 billion on R&D. There was only one firm from a developing country, Semiconductor Corporation (SMC), from China. Its spend in 2008–9 was $102 million, compared with more than $3 billion by each of the top twelve firms in the sector and $7.4 billion by the top-ranked firm, Nokia.

The world's top 100 brands are all owned by firms from high-income countries (Interbrand, 2011). Firms from the United States have fifty of the top 100 global brands and nine of the top ten. The only brand among the top 100 from a 'developing country' is Corona, is produced by the Mexican-based firm Grupo Modelo, which is 50 per cent owned by ABI.

Building business systems in developing countries
During the era of capitalist globalization, firms from the high-income countries not only invested heavily in each other's economies but also constructed comprehensive business systems in developing countries. Between 1990 and 2009 the inward stock of FDI in developing countries rose from $525 billion to $4.9 trillion, an increase from 14 per cent to 29 per cent of GDP. The inward flow of FDI into developing countries was mainly from firms from the developed countries. Although the outflow of FDI from developing countries grew substantially between 1990 and 2009, 84 per cent of the increase was from firms with their headquarters in the high-income countries (table 5). The total outward stock of FDI from developing countries amounts to just 17 per cent of that

Table 9 Stock of inward FDI in developing countries, 2000 and
2009 ($ billion)

	2000	2009	Increase, 2000–2009	
			$ billion	% total increase
Developing countries	1,728	4,893	3,165	100.0
Africa	154	515	361	11.4
Latin America/Caribbean	502	1,473	971	30.7
South Asia	30	218	188	5.9
South-East Asia	267	690	423	13.4
East Asia	710	1,561	851	26.9
of which: China	193	473	280	8.8
Oceania	4	12	8	0.3
West Asia	60	425	365	11.5
Southeast Europe and the CIS	61	497	436	–

Source: UNCTAD, 2010: Annex, Table 3.

from the developed countries, and the stock of inward
FDI is almost double the outward stock.

In the wake of the global financial crisis, global firms
from high-income countries face prolonged stagnation
in their home economies alongside continued robust
growth in developing countries.[19] Their focus is even
more strongly geared towards expanding their business
systems in developing countries, accentuating the trend
of the preceding period. The growth prospects for 'our'
leading firms depend critically on building their business

---

[19] It is uncertain if this will continue to be the case. Given the central role
of the high-income countries in the global business system, it is highly
likely that prolonged stagnation, or even outright recession, in those countries would have a severe negative impact on growth in the developing
countries.

positions inside 'them', the developing countries, with China at the forefront.

3

Who are They?

3.1 China catches up

China is at the forefront of the developing world in the era of capitalist globalization. In 1800 it accounted for around one-third of total global manufacturing output, compared with just 18 per cent in the West. In the ensuing 200 years there occurred the 'Great Divergence', as China's share of global GDP shrunk drastically. It is now commonplace to talk about a 'Great Convergence' taking place between China and the West.

The pace at which China's economy has caught up with the developed economies has astonished the world. By 2008, the country's Gross National Income (in PPP $) was larger than that of France, the UK and Germany combined and was 54 per cent of that of the USA. Its manufacturing output had risen to 85 per cent of that of the USA and was 61 per cent greater than that of Japan and over twice that of Germany (World Bank, 2010). In 2009 China overtook Germany to become the world's largest exporter. By 2010 it had forty-two firms in the Fortune 500 and twenty-three in the FT 500. The aggregate market capitalization of Chinese firms in the FT 500 was third, behind only the USA and the UK. During the global financial crisis China continued to grow strongly, while the high-income countries experienced their worst economic downturn since the 1930s. Indeed, China's bold decision to increase investment massively in 2008–10 was critically important for the global economy.

From the earliest days of China's economic reforms in the 1980s, the country's leadership has been committed to developing a group of globally competitive giant firms to match those from the high-income countries. As early as 1987 central policy-makers pointed out that 'the development of business groups is of profound long-term importance to the development of production capabilities and deepening the reform of the economic system'.

Constructing an industrial policy in China presented special challenges compared to the case with other late-comer countries, such as Japan and South Korea after 1950. China was attempting to reform a closed centrally planned economy with a negligible private sector. Japan and Korea were both bastions of the West's struggle against communism, and both had a massive US military presence. The West was prepared to accept a robust nationalist industrial policy in its East Asian partners who were in the front line in the struggle against communism. Communist China was viewed by the West as a profound ideological and military threat. Moreover, its attempt to construct an industrial policy has occurred in the midst of the era of capitalist globalization, which has produced unprecedented global industrial concentration of business power. The industrial policies pursued by Japan and Korea could not easily be transferred to China and they cannot easily be transferred to developing countries. From the outset in the late 1970s, China's economic reforms have been cautious and experimental, 'groping for stones to cross the river'. They have been viewed as part of a much wider process of 'system reform', with cautious experimentation, analysis and feedback into the ongoing process.

The essence of China's enterprise reform policy was crystallized in the slogan 'grasp the large, let go of the small'. By the late 1990s most of the small and medium-sized enterprise sector had been removed from state ownership, and a wide array of institutional structures emerged from the process. Although this was broadly referred to as 'privatization', the latter term does not fully capture the complexity of the process or its outcome. The non-state sector, which consists mainly of small and medium-sized enterprises, has made a vital contribution to China's growth. Removing the constraints over this sector unleashed the force of the country's vibrant tradition of entrepreneurship, which had been smothered since the mid-1950s under the administratively directed economy.[20]

---

[20] I use the term 'administratively directed economy' because the so-called planned economies were not planned in the strict sense, because they were unable to reach their stated goals in terms of technical progress and improvement in living standards. Rather, they were anarchic, unable to break out of the path-dependent pattern of development into which they were locked. It was only when they began to allow market forces to have a greater role in the economy that they were able to move away from this pattern of development (Nolan, 1995).

Alongside the rapid growth of the non-state sector, the commanding heights of the economy remained firmly under state ownership. A long series of experimental reforms attempted to create a group of globally competitive large enterprises. The leadership regarded this is as a central focus of the country's development strategy. In 1998 Vice-Premier Wu Bangguo summarized the government's policy as follows:

> International economic comparisons show that if a country has several large companies or groups it will be assured of maintaining a certain market share and a position in the international economic order. America, for example, relies on General Motors, Boeing, Du Pont and a batch of other multinational companies. Japan relies on six large enterprise groups and Korea relies on ten large commercial groupings. In the same way now and in the next century our nation's position in the international economic order will be to a large extent determined by the position of our nation's large enterprises and groups.

Initial cautious experiments in the 1980s increased enterprise autonomy and enhanced the right to retain profits and engage directly with the market. From the early 1990s onwards the reforms deepened. Large enterprises were transformed into corporate entities with diversified ownership. Minority equity shares were floated on domestic and international stock markets. In this process, large state-owned firms were subjected to public scrutiny, including meticulous examination of the floated companies by international accounting firms and investment banks. Joint ventures were established with leading international companies. A new generation of highly trained professional managers moved into senior positions. Extensive corporate restructuring took place through merger and acquisition. The number of 'national champion' firms was gradually reduced to around eighty super-large firms. Increasingly the corporate structure of China's giant enterprises resembled that of their international competitors. This was a remarkable achievement in terms of institutional transformation.

The main body of the national champion firms consisted of 'strategic industries'. These were broadly the same industries in which many high-income countries had established their own state-owned 'national champion' firms after the Second World War. Although the Western state-owned enterprises were mostly privatized after the 1970s, before this many of them had achieved significant scale and technical progress, which laid the foundation for their international success after privatization. China has constructed a large group of giant companies in key sectors, including telecoms (China Mobile, China Unicom and China Telecom); oil and chemicals (Sinopec, CNPC, CNOOC and Sinochem); aerospace (Aviation Industry of China (AVIC), Commercial Aircraft Company of China (COMAC) and China Aerospace Science and Technology Corporation); military and related equipment (China North and China South); automobiles and trucks (Shanghai Auto, Yiqi and Dongfeng); power equipment (Shanghai Electric, Harbin Electric and Dongfang Electric); metals and mining (Baosteel, Wugang (Wisco), Shenhua, China Minmetals and Aluminium Corporation of China); electricity generation and distribution (China Southern Power Grid,

National Grid (Guodian), Huaneng, Huadian and Datang); construction (China State Construction, China Rail Construction and China Construction); airlines (Air China, China Southern and China Eastern); and banking (Industrial and Commercial Bank of China, China Construction Bank, Bank of China, Agricultural Bank of China and Bank of Communications).

In these sectors, the state's majority equity share makes it difficult for international firms to expand within China through merger and acquisition, and the national champion firms benefit from their access to procurement contracts from government projects. Since these firms are all state-owned they are able to think in a long-term fashion. They can work together as a single team, sharing knowledge, supporting each other and buying each other's products. They can cooperate in the development of new technologies to meet China's needs for sustainable development in transport, buildings, electricity generation and transmission, and oilfield services. Each of these sectors has witnessed significant technical progress among domestic companies. China's booming economy has been based on an extremely high investment rate, which has created intense demand for output from the main body of the country's strategic industries. This has meant that revenues and profits at China's national champion firms have grown rapidly.

In key heavy industries, such as electricity generation, transport and oil, China's large state-owned enterprises have made substantial technical advances on the basis mainly of the huge growth in domestic demand.

In the 1990s, the international market for power stations manufacture was dominated by a handful of giant companies from the high-income countries, including Alstom, Mitsubishi, GE and Siemens. However, the growth of electricity production and distribution in China has far outpaced that in other parts of the world. Between 1990 and 2007 China accounted for one-third of the total global increase in electricity production. The Chinese government has ensured that the main body of the country's power equipment has been bought from domestic companies. Over four-fifths of electricity generation uses coal as the primary energy source, with a secondary role for hydro power and a fast-increasing role for nuclear power. The Chinese government has gradually tightened environmental regulations so that a growing share of the market has been supplied with less polluting larger power-generation units. The main domestic equipment companies (Harbin, Shanghai and Dongfang) have made steady technical progress. Harbin is the leading domestic company, with around one-third of the domestic coal-fired market and two-thirds of the hydro market. In the 1980s Harbin was only able to manufacture units of 30 to 200MW. In 1990 it installed its first sub-critical units of 300MW and 600MW, and in 2004 it installed its first super-critical unit of 600MW. It has supplied more than 250 units of 300MW and more than 200 units of 600MW to the domestic market, and recently supplied thirteen super-critical units of 1000MW. In addition to numerous small hydro-power units, it has supplied more than forty units of 700MW or above to different Chinese hydro projects, among them fourteen units to the giant Three Gorges project. Working closely with other elements in the Chinese engineering industry, Harbin has steadily increased its capability in the nuclear power sector, including the supply of sixteen units of third-generation AP1000 steam generators for China's nuclear power plants. It has exported power stations to Pakistan, Vietnam, Indonesia and Sudan. These have almost all been small units of less than 200MW. However, it has begun to export large units to Pakistan, and in 2010 it was announced that China's power equipment companies would be given massive orders to export plants to Indian power-generating companies.[21]

China has been at the forefront of the global expansion of high-speed rail travel. By 2010 it already had the world's largest high-speed rail network and plans to triple the high-speed capacity to 16,000 km by 2020. The high-speed train industry outside China is an oligopoly shared mainly between Siemens, Alstom, Bombardier and Kawasaki Heavy Industries, and these companies dominated the early phase of development in China. However, in order to gain access to the Chinese market, foreign firms were required to transfer technology to the indigenous Chinese companies, which rapidly upgraded their technology. Around 70 per cent of the new high-speed rolling stock and ancillary equipment is now purchased from domestic companies, principally the state-owned firms China North (CNR) and China South (CSR). Many commentators viewed the rapid technical progress of large Chinese state-owned companies in this sector as the beginning of a wider process of 'catch-up'

---

[21] It was reported that the total order could amount to as much as 22,000MW in generating capacity and be worth $7 billion, but it remains to be seen if this huge order comes to fruition.

in high-technology industries. China appeared to be poised to begin exporting high-speed trains on a large scale. In July 2011 the first export deal was announced, with the sale of a batch of trains to Malaysia. However, in the same month the Beijing to Shanghai high-speed train crashed, killing over forty people and injuring many more. It was widely suggested that this would greatly harm the possibility for the country's export not only of high-speed trains but also of other high-technology products. In fact, the long-term impact may be less severe than many analysts fear.[22] The rapid absorption and adaptation of advanced technologies in the high-speed train sector is a remarkable achievement for a developing country.

In the 1990s it seemed that China's oil companies might be split into smaller units, with great opportunities for global companies to penetrate the domestic market through joint ventures and acquisitions. Instead, in the late 1990s the oil industry went through a massive restructuring which resulted in two giant vertically integrated companies, CNPC and Sinopec, and one smaller company focusing on offshore oil and gas, CNOOC. So remarkable has the transformation been that, by 2010, PetroChina, the listed subsidiary of CNPC, became the world's largest listed oil company by market capitalization, surpassing even the US giant ExxonMobil. Unlike

---

[22] Japan's high-speed *shinkansen* train system has been in operation since 1964 without a single fatal accident. However, the worst high-speed rail crash in the world took place in Germany in 1998 at Eschede, in which 101 people were killed. The accident did little to dent either the export of high-speed trains from Germany or the image of Germany as a high-technology powerhouse.

the oil majors, which have outsourced a large share of their activities to specialist oilfield service companies, CNPC and Sinopec remain highly vertically integrated, including large research departments. In 2010 CNPC's R&D investment surpassed that of Shell, which had the largest R&D expenditure among the oil majors. Faced with stagnant domestic oil reserves, CNPC has made important technical progress in many areas, especially those connected with extracting oil from mature oilfields, and developing unconventional sources of oil and gas, such as coal-bed methane. Due to the rapid rise in domestic oil demand and the stagnation of domestic output, China's oil companies have pushed hard to expand their international operations, and in the process they have developed technical skills in the operation of oil and gas fields across a wide range of conditions. Between 2003 and 2010 the share of international production in CNPC's total oil output rose from 11 per cent to 26 per cent.

Later in this study I will examine the banking and aircraft industries. In both of these sectors China's state-owned enterprises have made remarkable achievements. A decade ago the country's banking industry was mired in massive bad debts, with a chorus of expert opinion calling for the break-up of the big banks. Within ten years the 'big four banks' had accomplished a comprehensive transformation. By 2010 China had nine banks in the FT 500, more than any other country, including the USA, and its banks occupied first, second and seventh positions in the FT's banking sector rankings. In the aircraft industry, China's attempt to build an indigenous large commercial aircraft, the Y-10, ended in failure in the 1980s. Its attempt to build medium-sized commercial aircraft in joint ventures with McDonnell Douglas/Boeing and Airbus also ended in failure in the late 1990s. Today, a decade later, China is producing its own regional jet, the ARJ21, and is well advanced in its plans to build a large commercial jet, the C919. It is determined to break the Boeing–Airbus global duopoly in large commercial aircraft.

In almost every discussion about China's 'catch-up' at the level of the firm, the case of Huawei arises. It has advanced from a minnow in the highly concentrated global telecom equipment industry to a giant firm with revenues in 2010 of $27.1 billion and an operating profit of over $4.3 billion. In the late 1990s Huawei comprehensively re-engineered the company, engaging IBM at great expense to lead the transformation from a technology-based to a customer-based approach. The process was so painful that its CEO likened it to 'cutting our feet to fit American shoes'. Huawei's foreign sales grew from $100 million in 1999 to almost $18 billion in 2010. Although its sales in developing economies are far greater than those in high-income countries, Huawei has made significant inroads into markets in the latter, especially in Europe. In 2005 it was certified as a qualified supplier to both BT and Vodafone, which required it to submit to the deepest scrutiny of its products and processes and all aspects of its performance, including not just technical issues but also its compliance with internationally accepted practices in terms of corporate social responsibility. Among large Chinese firms Huawei is unique in having met the most severe standards of global competition among customers in the high-income countries: it stands alone in being 'inside us'. It is unusual among large Chinese firms in terms of the continuity of its top management, its focus on core business, the high share of revenue allocated to R&D, the large share of its employees engaged in R&D, the large share of foreign workers among its employees, the open and transparent system of organization and remuneration of its workforce, the intellectual and physical attractiveness of the work environment, and the internationalization of its culture, including the use of English throughout the upper reaches of the company.

3.2 China is still far from 'catching up'

It is difficult for people in the high-income countries, who see constant images of 'China rising', to appreciate fully the fact that it is a developing country. China's population is 24 per cent larger than that of all the high-income countries together, and the intrinsic worth of each Chinese person is equal to that of an American or a European.

After more than two decades of rapid growth, there is still a wide development gap between China and the high-income countries (see table 10). China's national income is only one-fifth, and national income per person is only 16 per cent, of that of the high-income countries. Its exports are only 13 per cent of those of the high-income countries. It has just nine firms in the G1,400 list of companies and none in the top 100. Its household wealth is only 4 per cent of that of the high-income countries. Even after the latest round of reforms

Table 10 China and the world turned upside down

	China	High-income countries	China as a percentage of high-income countries
Population (million) (2008)	1,325	1,069	124
Gross national income (at official rate of exchange) (2008):			
• Total ($ billion)	3,881	42,415	9.2
• $ per person	2,940	39,687	7.4
Gross national income (PPP $) (2008):			
• Total ($ billion)	7,961	40,253	19.8
• $ per person	6,010	37,665	16.0
Household wealth ($ trillion, 2008)	3.41	87.0	3.9
Manufacturing value-added ($ billion, 2008)	1,488	6,040	24.6
Household consumption (billion PPP $, 2008)	2,707	24,957	10.8
Exports ($ billion, 2008)	1,428	11,060	12.9
FT 500 companies (2010)	23[a]	421	6.2
Fortune 500 companies (2010)	42[a]	440	7.7
Foreign direct investment: outward stock ($ billion, 2009)	230	16,011	1.4
Global top 1,400 companies by R&D spending (2008)	9	1,363	0.7
of which: top 100	0	100	0
IMF voting rights (%)[b]	3.65	59.5	6.1
	(6.07)	(55.3)	(11.0)
CO_2 emissions:			
• Total (million tons, 2006)	6,099	13,378	45.6
• Per capita (tons, 2006)	4.7	12.7	37.0

[a] Excluding Hong Kong.
[b] Figures in parentheses indicate post-2010 reform of voting rights. Under the 2010 agreement the United States' voting rights will fall from 16.7 per cent to 16.5 per cent; this still gives the United States a veto on major decisions, which require a 'super-majority' of 85 per cent.
Source: World Bank, 2010; BIS, 2009; International Monetary Fund; *Financial Times*; Fortune; BERR, 2008; BCG, 2009.

is completed, China's voting rights in the IMF will be only one-ninth of those of the high-income countries, even though its population is 24 per cent larger.

It cannot be assumed that China will grow indefinitely at its current high speed. The passage from lower middle income to upper middle income will be difficult. For several years China's leaders have stated the need to change the country's development model. On 16 March 2007, Premier Wen Jiabao stated the problem with disarming clarity: 'China's economy has maintained fast yet steady growth in recent years. However, this gives no cause for complacency, neither in the past, nor now, nor in the future. My mind is focused on the pressing challenges . . . There are structural problems in China's economy, which cause unsteady, unbalanced, uncoordinated and unsustainable development.'

China is fast approaching the end of the 'Lewis' phase of 'economic development with unlimited supplies of labour'. It faces the prospect of a sharp rise in the proportion of old people in the population, reflecting the drastic restriction on births from the late 1970s onwards under the one-child policy. These factors will fundamentally reshape Chinese political economy and are coming into play at an unusually early stage in China's development, in which it is still a lower middle income country. China is the first country in the modern world to have become so large without having achieved a high level of income per person and the first country to have passed through the 'Lewis phase' of development and to have become 'grey' before it has become rich. It faces deep challenges in order to contain and reverse the heavy damage to its physical environment.

This will involve large costs for the Chinese government and people.

During the process of 'reform and opening up', inequality of income and wealth have increased alarmingly, which threatens the country's social and political stability. The Gini coefficient of income distribution has risen from around 0.28 in the early 1980s to around 0.48 today (Luo and Nong, 2008). It is estimated that the top 0.1 per of households have 45.8 per cent of total household wealth (BCG, 2009). In other words, around 1.3 million out of China's total population of around 1.3 billion people have almost one-half of total household wealth. In the Western media there are constant reports about high-spending Chinese tourists. However, these are a tiny fraction of the population. The World Bank estimates that there still are almost 500 million people in China who live on less than $2.00 per day (World Bank, 2010: 92).

China faces an increasingly hostile international political environment. There is a wide range of popular books, newspaper articles and broadcasts warning about the threat posed by 'China's rise'. The interaction of the Western version of democracy with the dramatic changes in the mass media in recent decades has forced Western political leaders to be increasingly populist. They are threatened at every turn by the short-term sound bite and are in their turn preoccupied with influencing the mass media. Popular fears are stoked fiercely by the crisis in the political economy of the West. During the three decades of capitalist globalization, inequality of income and wealth rose sharply in most high-income countries. Consumption was sustained by the massive rise in personal debt, fuelled by a long-term asset bubble, with house price increases at the core. The eruption of the global financial crisis in 2008 brought this era to a crashing conclusion. Since then massive government debt has been added to the huge overhang of private debt. The high-income countries face the prospect of a long period of economic stagnation and possibly even worse. There are many scenarios for their evolution over the coming decade. Few of them are optimistic.

The role of international capital in China's 'reform and opening up' is debated intensely within the country. As a new generation of national leaders prepares to assume office, the Chinese Communist Party is reflecting deeply on the country's development path. China's political economy stands at a crossroads. The new generation of Chinese leaders will assume power at a time of deep systemic crisis in the West, and their interaction with those in power in the high-income countries at this difficult time is a tremendous leadership challenge.

3.3 China's deepening relationship with developing countries

Trade

China's trade relationship with developing countries has experienced a revolution in recent years. China is relatively poorly endowed with natural resources. Consequently its rapid industrial growth has stimulated an enormous increase in its imports of oil and gas, mining products and food from Africa and Latin

America, both of which are relatively well endowed with natural resources. The combined exports of Africa and Latin America to China rose twentyfold from \$5.4 billion in 1999 to \$108 billion in 2009 (SSB, 2000, 2010). This large rise in exports of mainly primary produce has made an important contribution to accelerated GDP growth in Africa and Latin America. China has become centrally important to the international trade of certain countries. For example, exports to China, which consist mainly of oil, account for 34 per cent of Angola's exports and 50 per cent of those of Sudan. China accounts for 15 to 16 per cent of the exports of Brazil and Chile. However, even though its significance has sharply increased, and in certain cases is critically important, China's role as a market for developing countries as a whole should not be exaggerated. It accounts for around 16 per cent of the exports of sub-Saharan Africa and around 8 per cent of the exports of Latin America as a whole.

At the same time as increasing their exports to China, developing countries have opened their markets to its imports. China's exports to Africa and Latin America increased from \$9.4 billion in 1999 to \$105 billion in 2009, rising from 4.8 per cent to 8.7 per cent of the total. Despite this large increase, they still amount to just one-sixth of China's combined exports to Europe, North America and Japan. Imports from China account for less than one-fifth of Africa's total and less than one-tenth of that of Latin America. However, due to the fact that the main body of China's exports to these regions consists of labour-intensive manufactures, across Africa and Latin America there is a wide perception that

71

the country's imports have helped to displace local labour in similar industries. China's exports to Africa and Latin America consists mainly of low-technology, labour-intensive manufactured goods,[23] especially consumer electronics, white goods, clothing and footwear, intended typically for sale to the relatively poor people who constitute the main body of the market in developing countries. Alongside the large rise in imports of goods from China, there has been a surge of Chinese business people who have migrated to developing countries. They act as the link in the chain of imports from China and are deeply embedded in the commercial network of developing countries. In many cities large commercial centres selling Chinese goods have grown up that are run entirely by Chinese business people. Sometimes they are on a massive scale with thousands of Chinese traders.

Infrastructure

Large Chinese infrastructure companies have emerged rapidly to play an important role in developing countries in the construction of roads, ports, railways, dams, harbours, bridges, hotels, sports stadiums, hospitals and houses. These have made an important contribution to economic development. They include both large centrally controlled companies, such as China Railway

---

[23] An important part of China's exports to developing countries consists of fake global brands produced mainly by small and medium-sized non-state firms. It is impossible to estimate exactly the share of the exports to developing countries that these occupy. Broadly speaking, the poorer the country and the lower the target group of consumers, the higher the share occupied by fake brands.

Construction, China Construction Corporation and China State Construction Engineering, and smaller infrastructure companies that are owned mainly by local governments. Chinese loans to the developing country governments, with a large share typically tied to procurement from Chinese companies, have been important in channelling contracts towards Chinese firms. The *Financial Times* estimates that in 2009–10 the China Development Bank and China Export-Import Bank lent a total of over $110 billion to developing country governments and companies, which exceeded the total of loans made by the World Bank in the same period (*Financial Times*, 17 January 2011). However, these figures are dwarfed by the size of private financial flows to developing countries. In 2008 financial flows to low- and middle-income countries amounted to a total of $826 billion, including foreign direct investment, bonds and bank lending (World Bank, 2010: 398).

Chinese firms have become extremely competitive in the infrastructure sector in developing countries. Its leading firms have acquired advanced skills in project management, including a high capability to build and design complex structures. They have a reputation not only for low costs but also for meeting project deadlines. They can achieve low costs on account of the large size of their domestic market in China and because they employ relatively low-cost Chinese workers who are brought in on a contract basis. The workers are reliable, hard-working and willing to live in simple conditions. Infrastructure construction is highly labour intensive, which creates severe challenges for Chinese firms in terms of labour organization in foreign countries. By employing mainly Chinese workers, China's infrastructure companies are able to avoid the difficulties of organizing a large local workforce who have a different language and culture.[24]

Anti-Chinese feelings

Anti-Chinese sentiment is a potent political weapon in many developing countries. The cultural impact of large numbers of Chinese workers in Africa and Latin America has been considerable and has provoked much discussion.[25] The real picture is complicated. The presence of large numbers of Chinese in the commercial sector is a source of resentment because of the perception that foreigners control a key part of a highly visible business activity in which there is close daily contact

---

[24] English is spoken over large parts of the developing world largely due to the influence of the British Empire, whereas knowledge of Chinese is almost non-existent.

[25] Many Western commentators view China's cultural impact on developing countries as a form of colonialism. One should be careful to place this discussion in a balanced historical context. Europeans colonized North America, dispossessing the native inhabitants. They were both directly and indirectly responsible for the destruction of most of the native population, who may initially have numbered as many as 15 million. Between the seventeenth and the early twentieth century, Europeans used their military might to conquer a large part of the world's population, turning most of Africa, South Asia and South East Asia into their colonial territories, and helped to destabilize and humiliate China through military invasion. European conquest of colonial territories was often violent and the dispossession of native people was frequently brutal, especially in the lands of permanent white settlement. The process of decolonization was not mainly completed until the 1960s, and involved violent confrontations between national liberation movements and the colonial powers, such as that in Vietnam between 1945 and 1954 and in Algeria between 1954 and 1962. China's cultural impact on Africa and Latin America bears no remote comparison with European colonialism.

with the local population. In the labour-intensive infrastructure sector, there is resentment at the fact that local workers feel they are perfectly capable of doing the same jobs, and there is a wide perception that unskilled wages are undercut by the low-cost Chinese workforce. Chinese infrastructure firms are often criticized because the workforce lives in isolated settlements with negligible outside contact. In the capital-intensive and highly skilled energy sector the situation is different. For example, in CNPC's oil operations in Sudan the majority of the most highly skilled jobs are filled by Sudanese oil engineers.

3.4 Oil companies and energy security

In both China and the West, energy security is a central issue in political economy. Energy security is intimately related to the industry's business structure as well as to wider issues of international relations, including military operations.[26] China has 13.3 per cent of the world's coal

[26] Most people in the Muslim world, and indeed in the world at large, believe the 'inconvenient truth' that both the First Gulf War and the invasion of Iraq in 2003 were closely connected with the United States' search for energy security, and that this was intimately connected with its wish to gain access to Iraqi oil for Western oil companies – and especially for American ones. In his memoirs published in 2007, Alan Greenspan, former chairman of the US Federal Reserve, shocked the US political establishment with his forthright statement: 'I am saddened that it is politically inconvenient to acknowledge what everyone knows: the Iraq war is largely about oil.'

During the era of capitalist globalization, the United States constructed a network of major military bases in the oil-rich Gulf region under the administration of a much enlarged Central Command ('Centcom'). They

reserves, but just 1.5 per cent of its natural gas reserves and a mere 1.1 per cent of its oil reserves (BP, 2011). While its oil production has increased very slowly, its oil consumption increased by 90 per cent between 2000 and 2010. By 2010 net oil imports amounted to 59 per cent of China's total consumption, and the prospect is for this to keep rising.

The state-owned national oil companies (NOCs) control around 90 per cent of the world's oil and gas reserves and account for around 75 per cent of global output. In 2007 the top ten NOCs had reserves of oil and gas that ranged from 39 billion barrels of oil equivalent (bboe) for Sonatrach (Algeria), to more than 300 bboe for both the Saudi Arabian Oil Company and the National Iranian Oil Company (*Oil and Gas*, 15 September 2008). China's largest oil company, CNPC, ranked thirteenth in the world, with reserves of 22 bboe – far behind the leading NOCs. The reserves of Sinopec and CNOOC together are estimated to total around 7 bboe, making a combined total of around 29 bboe of reserves for China's oil companies. In other words, the total oil and gas reserves of China's largest companies are around 28 bboe, far below even the tenth-ranked

include bases in Iraq and Kuwait (under 'Operation Iraqi Freedom'), Oman, Bahrain, Qatar and the United Arab Emirates. The US armed forces in the region total around 200,000. The US Fifth Fleet, with a complete carrier battle group, is stationed in Bahrain, and there is a total of six major US air force bases (two in Oman alone). In addition to the United States' own military capability, America's Muslim allies in the region have their own large armed forces, mainly supplied with US weaponry. Saudi Arabia has an air force which has over 80 F-15s, while Bahrain and Kuwait together have a similar number of American-supplied F-15s, F-16s and F-18s. In 2008, the Gulf States agreed a ten-year $20 billion arms deal with the United States.

NOC, Sonatrach, and a small fraction of those of Saudi Aramco or the Iranian National Oil Company.

The leading international oil companies from Europe and the USA have smaller reserves than the largest NOCs, but their collective reserves are far above those of China's oil companies. In the late 1990s there was a series of gigantic mergers and acquisitions in the oil industry, out of which the main features of the present structure of the Western 'oil majors' emerged. Among the most important of these were Exxon's acquisition of Mobil (for $86 billion), BP's acquisition of both Amoco (for $55 billion) and Arco (for $27 billion), Chevron's acquisition of Texaco (for $36 billion), Conoco's acquisition of Phillips (for $23 billion) and Total's acquisition of PetroFina (for $7 billion). The reserves of each of the six Western oil majors (ExxonMobil, BP, Chevron, Shell, ConocoPhillips and Total) are above 10 bboe, and total an estimated 68.4 billion bboe, far above the combined reserves of China's leading oil companies. In addition, there are eighteen medium-sized Western oil companies (of which ten are American) in the top fifty global oil companies, with total reserves of 42 bboe. In other words, the total reserves of Western oil companies are around 110 bboe, around four times the total reserves of China's oil companies.

The Western oil majors have built up powerful international reserves over many decades, so that their international reserves greatly exceed those of China's oil companies. They continually upgrade their asset base, selling off small, unprofitable reserves such as the declining North Sea fields and focusing on large, high-grade assets. They have played an important role in developing production in areas that are technically challenging, which has been a major factor driving forward technical progress in the industry. Their superior technology means that they are typically the partner of choice for NOCs when they are developing new fields that are technically challenging, such as Russia's vast Sakhalin projects. For example, Shell has a 27.5 per cent share in the Sakhalin I project, which will produce 395,000 barrels of oil equivalent per day (boe/d) at its peak – around the same output as the entire oil industry of Syria or Vietnam. ExxonMobil has a 30 per cent share in the Sakhalin II project, which produces 250,000 boe/d. In 2011, Russia's Rosneft agreed that ExxonMobil would be its partner in the development of its vast potential Arctic oilfields, which will involve a total investment of 'hundreds of billions of dollars'.

The Western oil majors are the lead operator in almost all the super-large projects in the world oil industry that are outside the territories of the leading NOC companies. For example, the massive Gorgon project in Australia will have a total investment of around $37 billion in the first phase alone.[27] Chevron is the lead operator, with a 47 per cent share, while ExxonMobil and Shell each have a 25 per cent share. Chevron is the lead operator also in the massive Wheatcroft natural gas project, also in Australia, that was approved in 2011. Chevron will invest $25 billion and will have a 73.6 per

---

[27] The Gorgon project got under way in 2009. It is Australia's largest-ever natural resource investment and one of the biggest oil and gas projects in the world. Chevron estimates that Gorgon's total gas reserves amount to 40 trillion cubic feet, equivalent to 6.7 bboe. Chevron believes that they will last for forty years and yield a total sales revenue of $500 billion.

cent share of the project. These mammoth projects will cement Chevron's position as the leading supplier of natural gas in the Asia-Pacific region.

The Western oil majors are the lead operators on almost all 'mega' oil projects (those with over 20,000 barrels per day) coming to fruition outside the territories of the leading NOCs in the near future. For example, in Angola, where China has increased its minority oil investments, there are ten 'mega' projects being completed between 2012 and 2015. Of these, Chevron is the lead operator on four, BP on three, Total on two and ExxonMobil on one. In Nigeria, where China also has increased its minority oil investments, there are nine mega oil projects coming to fruition in 2012–15, of which Shell is the lead operator on four, ExxonMobil on two, and Chevron, Total and Repsol on one each. Algeria, Indonesia, Kazakhstan, Papua New Guinea, Vietnam and Equatorial Guinea have a total of nine mega projects coming to fruition in 2012–15, of which ENI is the lead operator on three projects and Chevron on two, while ExxonMobil, Talisman, Noble and Anadarko[28] are each the lead operator on one.

From the 1950s until the 1980s the Chinese oil industry was cut off from the international economy. In the 1980s it was hoped that China would make major domestic oil and gas discoveries and that it would become a large-scale oil and gas exporter. Instead, China's reserves proved to be much smaller than was hoped and it has become increasingly dependent on

---

[28] Talisman, Anadarko and Noble Energy are independent oil operators.

energy imports. Up until the late 1990s the international operations of China's oil companies were of a negligible size compared to those of the Western oil majors. In the late 1990s CNPC's cumulative overseas investment totalled less than $1 billion, and its share of output from overseas reserves totalled only 1.9 million tons, around 1 per cent of domestic output. China's leading oil companies have a near monopoly in the protected domestic market, which has enabled them to achieve large sales and profits expansion. However, in international markets they are squeezed between the established NOCs and the powerful long-established international position of the oil majors.

China's state-owned oil companies, CNPC, Sinopec and CNOOC, have begun seriously to develop their international operations only in recent years. In 2005, amid a storm of political controversy, CNOOC was rebuffed in its attempt to acquire the medium-sized American oil company Unocal. This demonstrated decisively that leading Chinese oil companies could not expect to acquire or merge with Western oil companies and thereby expand their reserves and upgrade their technological level.[29] Following the failure of CNOOC's attempt to acquire Unocal, Chinese expansion in the high income countries has been confined almost entirely to taking minority positions, especially in the oil sands industry, where they have invested a total of around $10

[29] In 2010 the joint acquisition by CNPC and Shell of Australia's Arrow Energy in a 50:50 deal worth $3.4 billion may turn out to be a milestone in the relationship of China's oil companies with the oil majors. However, the relationship between China's leading oil companies and the Western oil majors from the high-income countries is complicated and unresolved.

billion in North American companies.[30] In 2009, at a single stroke, ExxonMobil vastly increased its presence in the North American oil sands industry by the acquisition of XTO for $41 billion. Following the transaction, ExxonMobil became the USA's number one natural gas producer. Between 2008 and 2010 Shell invested a total of $14 billion in acquisitions to establish a leading position in North American shale gas.[31]

The main path for international expansion of China's oil companies has been through minority investments in oil and gas assets in developing countries. Their equity shares are scattered across many countries, but the main concentration is in four countries – Kazakhstan, Sudan, Venezuela and Angola. Most of the international acquisitions by China's oil companies in recent years have been small-scale investments in minority shares. The International Energy Association (IEA, 2011) lists a total of forty-one international oil and gas acquisitions by Chinese oil companies since 2001. Of these, twenty-two were less than $1 billion and seventeen were between $1 billion and $5 billion. Just two were over $5 billion, the largest of which was $8.8 billion. In 2009 China's international oil and gas acquisitions

[30] In 2010 Sinopec invested $4.65 billion to acquire ConocoPhillips's 9 per cent stake in Syncrude, a Canadian oil sands firm. In 2011 CNOOC invested $2.1 billion to acquire a 35 per cent stake in Canada's Long Lake oil sands project. In the USA in 2010 CNOOC invested $2.1 billion to acquire a 33.3 per cent share of the Eagle Ford Shale project and $1 billion to acquire a 33.3 per cent stake in Chesapeake Energy's DJ Basin and Powder River Basin projects.
[31] Shell acquired Duvernay (for $5.9 billion), East Resources (for $4.7 billion) and Eagle Ford (for $3.5 billion). Shell predicts that its North American 'tight gas' production could reach 400,000 boe/d by 2020.

totalled $18 billion, a large increase compared with those of previous years. However, the global total of oil and gas acquisitions in 2009 was $144 billion, which means that China's share was just 13 per cent. The largest Chinese international acquisition is dwarfed by a single recent large investment by one of the oil majors, such as ExxonMobil's $41 billion acquisition of XTO in 2009 or Chevron's combined investments in the Gorgon and Wheatcroft projects, which amount to around $40 billion.

In the face of the slow and difficult process of increasing its international reserves through small-scale acquisitions, China has made a series of 'loans for oil'. The IEA estimates that China's total loans for oil have amounted to $77 billion, which account for a large part of its loans to developing countries. In 2009–10 the 'loans for oil' included $25 billion to Russian oil and pipeline companies (Rosneft and Transneft respectively), $10 billion to Brazil's Petrobras for oilfield development, $5 billion to Kazakhstan, $6 billion to Angola, and $4 billion to Venezuela's PDVSA. Although the loans have helped to increase the country's oil security, they have done little to advance the international competitive position of China's oil companies through expanded international operations.

There is still a wide gap between the international operations of China's oil companies and those of their international competitors from the high-income countries. The international assets of the leading oil majors, such as Shell, BP, ExxonMobil, Total and Chevron, dwarf their domestic operations, with 70 to 80 per cent of their assets located in foreign countries. In 2009 their international assets ranged from $96 billion for ENI to $222 billion for Shell. Even though the share of CNPC's international operations is rising fast, in 2010 its international oil output amounted to only 26 per cent of its total output and international gas production to 13 per cent of the total. Sinopec is the leading oil refiner in China, but its international oil production is less than 5 per cent of its total output.

Unlike the oil majors, China's large oil companies are vertically integrated, including not only oil and gas production and marketing but also chemical production, petrol stations, pipeline construction and a full range of oilfield services, as well as the manufacture of refineries and petroleum equipment. Their international oilfield service operations are small compared with those of leading specialist companies, such as Schlumberger, Baker Hughes and Halliburton. In 2010 just 9 per cent of CNPC's drilling operations, 7 per cent of its well-logging operations and 2 per cent of its downhole operations were overseas. The international scale of its equipment manufacture is small compared with that of specialist global companies. CNPC's exports of petroleum equipment in 2010 totalled $1.6 billion, equivalent to the international sales of a medium-sized global company in the sector. In the chemical sector China's oil companies face intense international competition from giant specialist chemical companies, such as Bayer, BASF and Dow, each of which has R&D expenditure that exceeds that of CNPC's total R&D expenditure.

3.5 Multinational companies 'going in' to China

It would be a serious misunderstanding of the strategy of multinational companies to exaggerate the significance of China compared with other parts of the developing world. For example, the growth of inward FDI into Latin America and the Caribbean, mainly from the leading international firms, has outpaced that into China by a wide margin. The stock of inward FDI in China is less than one-third of that in Latin America and the Caribbean (table 9). China's large firms have only just begun their process of 'going out'. Outside China they must confront global giant firms with well-established production systems across the world, in both high-income and developing countries. Leading businesses from the high-income countries have been 'going out' for the whole era of modern capitalist globalization.

For example, US-based Caterpillar is the world's leader in construction and earth-moving equipment.[32] In 2009 CAT's North American revenue amounted to $16.7 billion, compared with $4.5 billion from Latin America, $14.3 billion from Europe, Africa and the Middle East, and $6.4 billion from the Asia-Pacific region. The combined employment of CAT and its dealer network totalled 104,000 in North America, 31,400 in Latin America, 55,000 in Europe, Africa and the Middle East, and 32,800 in Asia-Pacific. Praxair is a US-based company of which few people have heard, but it is representative of leading firms within the global

---

[32] In 2000 CAT acquired Bucyrus for $7.6 billion, which greatly strengthened its position across the range of mining equipment.

value chain. It occupies a key position within the supply chain of many different sectors, supplying industrial gases around the world. In 2009 its assets were distributed as follows: $7.2 billion in North America, $3.2 billion in Latin America, $2.4 billion in Europe, and $1.9 billion in Asia. It employed 10,183 people in the USA and 16,078 people in other parts of the world.

At the same time that Chinese firms are trying to 'go out', they must also face global companies who carry the competitive struggle deep into the Chinese economy, with their international production systems as the foundation. In terms of military strategy, the leading multinational companies are taking the 'war' into the enemy's camp, 'going in' to China in order to weaken the fighting capability of indigenous firms before they can build their capability outside the country. The 'war' is made more complex by the weakening relationship of the multinational companies with the political economy of their home country.

China is a key part of the growth strategy of most multinational companies. It has consistently been the largest recipient of inward FDI among developing countries. Although the role of foreign firms is tightly constrained in strategic industries, over large parts of the Chinese business system, international companies have rapidly expanded their investments, employment and sales, occupying important positions within these sectors. They view expansion in China as critical to their long-term prospects. The rapid growth of the Chinese economy since the eruption of the global financial crisis has helped greatly to sustain the prospects for global companies based in high-income countries.

Despite the attenuation of the relationship of global firms with their home country, they urge their governments to lobby China to open up their economy further to investment by international firms. They argue passionately that China must establish a 'level playing field' for international firms. They complain bitterly about the 'unfairness' of China's industrial policy to nurture its national champion firms. In fact, in the view of some Western CEOs, China is a more friendly environment for business expansion even than the USA: 'It's like a well-managed company, China. You have a one-stop shop in terms of the Chinese foreign investment agency and local governments are fighting for investments with each other' (Muhtar Kent, chief executive of the Coca-Cola Company, quoted in the *Financial Times*, 27 September 2011).

I will now look at the examples of the expansion in China of the business system of selected American and German firms.

The United States has by far the largest stock of global outward FDI, amounting to 27 per cent of the total for all developed countries in 2009 (table 5). It has a total of nearly 60,000 investment projects in China. In 2008 the sales volume of these enterprises totalled $147 billion, their export volume was $72 billion and their profits were nearly $8 billion (Wen, 2010). The US–China Business Council estimates that US companies have almost $100 billion in FDI in China. As can be seen from the following selected examples, China forms a key part of the global business system of a large fraction of America's top international companies across a wide array of sectors, from iPads to fried chicken.

Leading American global companies are deep 'inside' China:

- *United Technologies* In 2010 United Technologies' China business employed over 17,000 people and had revenues of over $3 billion. Its Otis division occupies around 25 per cent of the Chinese elevator market and its Carrier division occupies around one-fifth of the Chinese market for commercial air-conditioning systems. Both United Technologies and GE (below) also have a key position in the Chinese aerospace industry.
- *Apple* China is an important market for Apple products, growing at fantastic speed thanks to 'Apple mania'. In the first three quarters of 2011, its sales in Greater China reached $8.8 billion. China is crucial for Apple's supply chain. A large share of the assembly of Apple products is undertaken by Foxconn (Taiwan), which has over 900,000 employees in China and plans to increase this number to 1.3 million within two years. As well as assembling Apple products it assembles products for other leading US high-technology companies, including HP, Dell and Cisco.
- *Dow Chemical* Dow has twenty manufacturing sites in China, which employ nearly 4,000 people. In 2010 it had sales revenue of $3.7 billion in the country, making it Dow's second largest market.
- *General Electric* GE is investing over $2 billion in its China business in 2010–12, and in 2010 its sales there amounted to $6 billion.
- *General Motors* In 2010 GM sold 2.4 million

vehicles in China, which exceeds its US sales. It vies with VW for the top position in the Chinese automobile market. GM has eleven plants in China employing 32,000 people, compared with 52,000 in the USA, and is investing $5 to $7 billion there in the next five years, with the goal of doubling capacity to 3.7 million units.

- *Johnson Controls* Johnson Controls is the world leader in the manufacture of auto seats and batteries. China is its fastest growing market, with 18,000 employees in forty-seven manufacturing plants and revenues of over $3 billion. It occupies around 45 per cent of the Chinese market for auto seats.

- *Caterpillar* CAT is the world leader in construction equipment, with Komatsu (Japan) and Volvo (Sweden) its main competitors. China is CAT's largest market for construction equipment. It has thirteen manufacturing sites there, employing 8,500 people. Its 2010 revenues from China were almost $4 billion. In addition, there are ninety CAT dealers across the country, employing several thousand people; CAT estimates that its supply chain employs around 70,000 people. Local companies such as SANY and Xugong have a substantial share of low-technology equipment, but CAT, along with Komatsu and Volvo, has a commanding position in the large, high-technology construction equipment market. It is 'pouring investment into China', investing around $1 billion in the next three to four years: 'nothing short of being number one in China will do'.

- *Nike* Nike is the world's leading sports shoe company, with a global market share of around one-third.

It employs 34,000 people globally, but it employs around 500,000 people indirectly in independent factories around the world to which it subcontracts most manufacturing. China is Nike's biggest single source of supply, employing 176,000 people working in subcontracted factories.

- *Procter & Gamble* P&G is a global leader in a wide array of household goods. It employs over 7,000 people in China, where it has sales revenue of $5 billion.

- *Coca-Cola* China is Coca-Cola's fastest-growing market. Since 1979 the company has invested over $5 billion there. It has forty-one bottling plants, which employ over 48,000 people. In 2009–11 it invested $3 billion in its business in the country, and it plans to invest a further $4 billion in 2012–14. In addition to the direct employees working for Coca-Cola and its bottlers, the company has a long supply chain, including packaging, ingredients and transport, with an estimated workforce of over 400,000 people.

- *Pepsico* Pepsico has twenty-seven plants in China manufacturing soft drinks and snacks, with 20,000 employees. It is making investments of almost $4 billion in China between 2008 and 2013, which will add a further ten to twelve new plants across the country.

- *Yum!* Yum! Brands has almost 4,000 quick-service restaurants (QSRs) in China, most of which are KFC brand. It employs around 230,000 people, mainly young people working part-time, compared with around 65,000 in the USA. It estimates that its market share in the QSR segment in China is around 40 per cent, and its sales revenue in 2010 was $4.1 billion – one-fifth greater than its US sales: 'We think China is the Number 1 growth opportunity for Yum! in the twenty-first century and we love our leading position in this huge dynamic market.' It sources almost all of its ingredients locally and has over 500 suppliers.

- *McDonald's* McDonald's is the second largest QSR chain in China, with over 1,300 stores that employ more than 80,000 people. It is in the process of expanding to around 2,000 stores by 2013, which will require an additional 50,000 employees.

- *WalMart* WalMart's domestic US employment and sales dwarf those outside the USA. However, its Chinese business is growing rapidly, with 95,000 employees and revenues of $7 billion in 2010. China is critically important within its overall procurement. WalMart's global revenues in 2010 reached $408 billion. It is estimated that over 60 per cent of the company's total procurement is imported, and in 2002 WalMart set up its global procurement headquarters in Shenzhen. China is much the biggest source of its imported products, which include food, clothing, footwear, garden equipment and electrical products. WalMart is reluctant to estimate the number of people who work for its suppliers in China; however, it estimates that it purchases agricultural products from around 1 million farmers. The total number of people employed in the WalMart supply chain in China is likely to exceed by far that of any other American company.

Germany's stock of FDI in China is much less than that of the USA. However, German firms have rapidly increased their investment in China and the total FDI of German firms stands at around $20 billion. A group of giant German firms with global operations occupy a central position in several sectors of the Chinese system:

- *Volkswagen* VW stands at the forefront of the German penetration of the Chinese market. It has two giant subsidiaries, in Shanghai and Changchun respectively.[33] They employ 53,000 people between them. In 2010 VW's operations in China had revenues of $42.4 billion, comparable to those of a giant global company such as Renault, Dow Chemical or Pepsico. Profits from its China business reached €2.63 billion, more than one-third of VW's total profits of €6.84 billion. VW and GM are the most powerful firms in the Chinese auto industry, and China is VW's largest and fastest-growing market. In 2010 it sold 1.9 million cars and occupied around 17 per cent of the Chinese market. It plans to invest $13.9 billion in China in 2011–15 'in order to expand and consolidate its leading position'.
- *Bosch* Bosch is by far the world's most powerful firm in the auto components sector. It is rapidly

---

[33] These are joint ventures with Shanghai Auto and First Auto Works respectively. However, the management, brands, vehicle development, technology and strategy are firmly in VW's hands. 'SAIC' is technically a Fortune 500 company, but its revenues are almost entirely from its two joint ventures, one with VW and the other with GM. It has a limited capacity to compete as an independent auto manufacturer within China, let alone on the international stage.

building its business system in China alongside the expansion of global systems integrators, to which it is a key sub-systems supplier; it employs over 26,000 people, and in 2010 its revenues reached $5.8 billion. It is investing heavily in China and plans that employment there will rise to 50,000 by 2015.

- *Siemens* Siemens's portfolio of businesses in China includes power, medical and transport equipment, in each of which it has a leading global position. China also constitutes an increasingly important base for sourcing key components and sub-systems. Its Chinese operations employ 33,600 people and had revenues of $8.1 billion in 2010.

- *BASF* BASF has played an important role in expanding the supply of chemicals in China. Since 1990 it has invested $5.3 billion in twenty-six wholly owned subsidiaries and fourteen joint ventures, amounting to around one-fifth of total German FDI in the country. Some of these are enormous investments, such as the $2.9 billion joint venture (50:50) with Sinopec in Nanjing. BASF employs 7,000 people in China, and in 2010 the revenues from its Chinese operations reached $8.1 billion. It plans to invest more than $3 billion in the next few years, including an investment of $1.7 billion in the world's biggest MDI[34] plant in Chongqing and a further $1 billion in the Nanjing joint venture.

- *ThyssenKrupp* ThyssenKrupp is a world leader in stainless steel for autos and domestic appli-

---

[34] Methylene Diphenyl Diisocyanate (*sic*), which is usually abbreviated as 'MDI'.

ances, elevators and auto components. It has 11,000 employees in China, with revenues of \$2.8 billion in 2010.

- *Adidas* Adidas and Nike compete intensely. Between them they account for over one-half of the global market for athletic footwear, sports apparel and related products. In 2010 Adidas's global revenues reached \$16.5 billion. Subcontracted suppliers, mainly in Asia, produced almost all of its products. In 2010 subcontractors in China supplied Adidas with 85 million pairs of sports shoes and 108 million pieces of apparel. At least 100,000 people are employed there making Adidas sports goods.

Multinational firms have made a critically important contribution to China's growth and modernization. They have been central to its ability to benefit from the 'advantages of the latecomer', especially through the application of the world's leading-edge technologies in almost every sector, from aircraft to soft drinks. Foreign-invested firms account for around 28 per cent of the country's overall industrial value-added (see table 11). Their contribution is especially important in high technology. Foreign-invested enterprises account for around two-thirds of the overall value-added in high-technology industries, and within the sector they accounted for 71 per cent of total value-added in the electronic and telecommunications equipment sector and 91 per cent in the computer and office equipment sector. They account for 55 per cent of China's total exports and for 90 per cent of exports of high-technology products, including 99 per cent of its exports of computers and office

Table 11 Foreign-invested enterprises in the Chinese economy, 2007–9

Sector	Share of foreign-invested enterprises (%)
Industrial value-added[a]	28
of which:	
• Output from high-technology industries[b]	66
of which:	
• Medical, precision and optical instruments[b]	43
• Electronic and telecoms equipment[b]	71
• Computers and office equipment[b]	91
Total exports[c]	55
of which:	
• New and high-technology products	90

[a] 2009.
[b] 2007.
[c] 2008.
Source: Gao, 2011; SSB, 2010; Steinfeld, 2010.

equipment (Gao, 2011). It is estimated that foreign-invested enterprises employ 37 per cent of China's total-high technology workforce and 41 per cent of its scientists and engineers (Steinfeld, 2010: 161). As can be seen from the examples given above, the numbers of people working in China within the value chain of foreign firms is extremely large and beyond easy calculation.

China is unique among large latecomer countries in the degree of importance of foreign firms in its modernization and national economic catch-up. It is remarkable that such an exceptionally high degree of openness has occurred under Communist Party rule, which contradicts the predictions of almost all international experts on the 'transition' from central planning.

Table 12 Balance between China's inflows and outflows of FDI ($ million)

	2000	*2005*	*2007*	*2009*
FDI inflows	40,715	72,406	83,521	95,000
FDI outflows	916	12,261	22,469	48,000
Outflows minus inflows	*–39,799*	*–60,145*	*–61,052*	*–47,000*
FDI inward stock	193,348	272,094	327,087	473,083
FDI outward stock	27,768	57,206	95,799	229,600
Outward stock minus inward stock	*–165,580*	*–214,888*	*–231,288*	*–243,483*

Source: UNCTAD, 2010: Annex, tables 1–4.

3.6 Chinese firms 'going out' of China into the high-income economies: 'I have you within me but you do not have me within you'

China's stock of outward FDI increased eightfold, from $27 billion in 2000 to $230 billion in 2009 (UNCTAD, 2010: Annex), which has inspired intense media discussion and the widespread perception that China is 'buying the world'. It seems that China's 'going out' policy for its giant state-owned firms has taken off. This perception has strongly influenced the view that firms from developing countries generally are catching up with and overtaking those from the high-income countries on a widespread basis.

In fact, there has been a large and persistent 'deficit' in China's FDI, with inflows consistently exceeding outflows. The excess of China's inward stock of FDI over its outward stock increased from $165 billion in 2000 to $243 billion in 2009 (see table 12).

China's firms are at the very earliest stage of building

Table 13 Globalization and FDI: outward stock of FDI, 1990 and 2009 ($ billion)

	1990	2009
Developed economies	1,942	16,010
of which:		
• USA	732	4,303
• UK	229	1,652
• Germany	152	1,378
• France	112	1,720
• Netherlands	107	851
• Australia	31	344
• Denmark	7	216
Developing and transition economies	145	2,691
of which:		
• Singapore[a]	8	213
• Russia	negl.	249
• Taiwan[a]	30	181
• Brazil	41	158
• China	4	230 (76)[b]
• India	negl.	77

[a] The World Bank categorizes both Singapore and Taiwan as high-income economies.

[b] Excluding Hong Kong and Macao; 67 per cent of China's outward stock of FDI is in Hong Kong and Macao (SSB, 2009: tables 17–20).

Source: UNCTAD, 2010, Annex.

global production systems. In 2009 the country's outward stock of FDI was 27 per cent of that of the Netherlands, 17 per cent of that of Germany, 13 per cent of that of France, 14 per cent of that of the UK, and 5 per cent of that of the USA (see table 13). It amounted to less than one-fiftieth of that of the high-income countries as a whole. China's total stock of outward FDI (excluding Hong Kong) is just one-fifth of the value of GE's foreign assets ($401 billion) or one-half of

Table 14 Distribution of China's outward stock of FDI, 2009 ($ billion)

Region/country	$ billion	%
Total	245.8	100
of which:		
• Hong Kong/Macao	166.3	67.7
• Africa	9.3	3.8
• Latin America	30.6	12.4
of which:		
• Cayman Islands	13.6	5.5
• Virgin Islands	15.1	6.1
High-income countries[a]	27.1	11.0
of which:		
Europe	8.7	3.5
• France	0.2	negl.
• Germany	1.1	0.4
• UK	1.0	0.4
North America	5.2	2.1
• USA	3.3	1.3
Japan	0.7	0.3
Singapore	4.9	2.0
Korea	1.2	0.5
Oceania	6.4	2.6

[a] Excluding Hong Kong.
Source: SSB, 2010: 257.

ExxonMobil's ($161 billion). Its total global stock of FDI in the manufacturing sector is just $14 billion (SSB, 2010), on a par with the international assets of a single medium-sized global company or the equivalent of a single acquisition by a leading US multinational, such as Kraft's recent $19 billion acquisition of Cadbury, the iconic British confectionery company.

China's outward FDI in the high-income countries is negligible, and 68 per cent of it is in Hong Kong/Macao (table 14); only 11 per cent – just $27 billion – is in the high-income countries, compared with an inward stock of nearly $500 billion, most of which is from the high-income countries. In other words, the high-income countries' stock of FDI in China is almost twenty times as large as China's FDI stock in the high-income countries. China's stock of outward FDI in the USA is $3.3 billion. In both Germany and the UK it is around $1.1 billion, while in France it is just $0.2 billion. The USA's stock of FDI in China (i.e., around $100 billion) is thirty times as large as China's stock of FDI in the USA, while Germany's stock in China (i.e., $20 billion) is around twenty times as large as China's stock in Germany.

Chinese firms have been conspicuously absent from major international mergers and acquisitions, which is centrally important for building a global business system. China's giant banks played no role whatsoever in the massive round of mergers and acquisitions during the global financial crisis. There have been only a tiny number of significant international acquisitions by Chinese companies. In 2005 Lenovo acquired IBM's PC division for $1.75 billion. This was highly significant and has helped make Legend a global force in the PC market. However, the reason that IBM was willing to sell the division is its low profitability coupled with intense competition in the sector. In September 2011, HP, the world's largest producer of PCs, announced that it was planning to spin off its PC division on account of its low profitability. It was not until 2010 that a Chinese company made another significant international acquisition, when the auto manufacturer Geely acquired Volvo Cars for $1.8 billion. Volvo Cars was a loss-making division within Ford. Nevertheless, this may be an astute acquisition and help Geely to build its brand within China as well as deepening its understanding of international markets. Although these acquisitions may make good commercial sense, neither is a large acquisition in global terms, and they stand out as exceptions to the rule in terms of China's international acquisitions. In the same week that these lines are being written (late September 2011) SABMiller announced its $10.4 billion acquisition of Fosters, Australia's leading brewing company, and United Technologies made an offer of $18.4 billion to acquire Goodrich (USA), the world's leading supplier of landing gear for commercial aircraft. These relatively minor acquisitions in global terms attracted negligible comment in the international financial press, but each of them far exceeded either of the two iconic Chinese international acquisitions of the last decade.

The efforts of China's large firms to acquire businesses in the high-income countries have mostly ended in failure. In June 2005 the third largest Chinese oil company, CNOOC, launched a bid of $18.5 billion to acquire the medium-sized US oil company Unocal. Zhou Shouwei, the president of CNOOC, said: 'If the bid succeeds CNOOC's business will be transformed from a Chinese into a global enterprise.' In fact the bid was greeted with a storm of opposition in the US media. In early July the US House of Representatives voted by 398 to 15 to call on the US government to review it on the grounds that it constituted a 'threat to US national security'. On 3 August 2005 CNOOC withdrew its bid. Subsequently, Unocal was acquired by Chevron.

A succession of possible international acquisitions by Huawei were all abandoned. In 2005 it was rumoured that it was in negotiations to acquire Marconi, the venerable but loss-making UK telecoms equipment maker. This prompted intense discussion in the UK mass media and rumours that the deal would be referred to the US government's Committee on Foreign Investment in the United States (CFIUS). Huawei made no formal offer to acquire Marconi, and eventually it was sold to Ericsson for \$2.1 billion. In 2010 Huawei made a bid to acquire the tiny niche American telecoms software company 3Leaf for \$2 million, a minuscule transaction in global terms. The deal was blocked by CFIUS on national security grounds.

An alternative to full-scale takeover is the acquisition by Chinese companies of substantial minority shares in leading Western companies. In 2007–8 it was proposed that Huawei would acquire 3Com, the US telecoms equipment company, jointly with the US private equity firm Bain Capital. Despite the fact that Huawei would own only a small minority share, and despite the fact that 3Com is a relatively small company, the proposal led to US media furore focusing on Huawei's 'threat to US national security', and the case was referred to CFIUS. Before a formal ruling was reached, the acquisition offer was withdrawn by Bain and Huawei. In 2010 HP acquired 3Com for \$2.2 billion.

In February 2009 there was a second large-scale effort by a leading Chinese company to invest in a substantial minority stake in a global company. A deal was agreed between Chinalco, the leading Chinese mining company, and Rio Tinto, the Australian-based global mining giant.[35] Chinalco would make a $19.5 billion investment to acquire an 18 per cent equity share of Rio Tinto.[36] It would be allowed to nominate two non-executive directors to the Rio Tinto board, and the companies were to set up a joint venture to develop new mines outside China. The agreement was path-breaking in relation to the international expansion route of giant Chinese state-owned enterprises and their relationship with the leading international companies. The Australian government delayed giving a ruling on the decision. By early June 2009 the Australian Foreign Investment Review had still not completed its investigation. In the meantime opposition grew from both shareholders and politicians. High-profile Australian politicians opposed it on the grounds that it would allow a foreign state-backed enterprise to own a strategic stake in the country's biggest natural resource asset and would allow a member of the Chinese Communist Party to sit on the Rio Tinto board. Amid heavy pressure, the board of Rio Tinto decided to abandon the deal before the ruling by the Australian government. The decision caused a furore in China, including the internet, with sentiments such as: 'Rio Tinto is like a dishonourable woman, only interested in Chinalco's money.'[37]

One can always speculate about the future. However, up until this point, Chinese firms have been extremely

[35] In fact, Rio Tinto is jointly listed in both the UK and Australia, but a large fraction of its physical assets are in Australia.

[36] Chinalco had already acquired a 9 per cent stake in Rio Tinto, so the proposal was to raise its stake from 9 per cent to 18 per cent.

[37] In fact, Chinalco remained a major shareholder in Rio Tinto and has a number of significant international projects in which it cooperates.

cautious in their international mergers and acquisitions, as well as in their international 'greenfield' investments. China's 'going out' strategy has advanced furthest in the critically important energy sector. However, even here its leading firms have proceeded circumspectly in their international expansion in both developing and high-income countries. They have far to go before they catch up with the global operations of the oil majors, the leading oil service companies or the chemical companies. China's large firms from different industries have failed in several efforts to acquire international companies, mainly on account of political obstacles to 'their' firms acquiring 'our' firms. The acquisitions that they have made are small in scale compared with the routine mergers and acquisitions that are made continually by the world's leading companies. China's large firms are far removed from the global production systems that the world's leading firms, mostly with their headquarters in the high-income countries, have established during the three decades of modern capitalist globalization.

3.7 Constraints on China 'buying the world'

How large are China's foreign exchange reserves?
The perception of most Western commentators and, indeed, ordinary citizens is that China has 'enormous' foreign exchange reserves that it is using to 'buy the world'. It is true that China has very large reserves, totalling $3,200 billion by June 2011, by far the largest in the world. However, this can be looked at from a variety of perspectives.

China is still a developing country. The 'umbrella' of its foreign exchange reserves has to 'shelter' 1.3 billion people. In mid-2011 its reserves amounted to $2,459 per person, compared with $6,356 per person for Korea, $8,889 for Japan, $39,601 for Hong Kong and $60,571 for Singapore. The Asian financial crisis deeply scarred East Asian countries. Since then they have mostly built up their foreign exchange reserves as a form of insurance against an international financial crisis rather than as a vehicle for international business expansion. The State Administration of Foreign Exchange (SAFE) has the weighty responsibility of managing China's foreign exchange reserves: 'Since China is a large developing country, maintaining sufficient foreign exchange reserves is of great significance to ensure international liquidity, enhance the capability to respond to risk, and safeguard the economic and financial security of the nation' (www.safe.gov.cn, 2011). China's policymakers were for many years deeply concerned that the deregulation of the Western financial system through 'regulatory capture' by giant global banks would cause a global financial crisis. It pursued an extremely conservative domestic regulatory regime completely at odds with that in the West, and in the face of heavy international criticism of their approach. In fact, their fears proved to be well founded.

The current global financial crisis is far from over. It has already had a profound effect on China, leading it greatly to increase bank lending in order to stimulate the economy in the face of the collapse in external demand in 2008–9. It remains to be seen what long-term impact this will have on the country's banking system. Its leaders are vigilant, fully aware that the international crisis could deepen, which would have profound implications for China. Under these circumstances, China's foreign exchange reserves must be managed prudently, with a large share allocated to secure, liquid assets, even if the return on these is much less than on alternative investments. This task has become even more difficult on account of the sovereign debt crisis in the West.

China's total foreign exchange reserves are small in comparison with the funds managed by Western asset managers. In 2009 the world's top 500 asset managers had a total of $62 trillion of assets (Towers Watson, 2010). Within this total, US asset managers had a total of $30.6 trillion and European asset managers had $24.1 trillion, totalling $54.7 trillion, while asset managers in developing countries had just $2.5 trillion under management. The top firm, BlackRock, had $3.3 trillion, exceeding China's total foreign exchange reserves today. Funds come in all shapes and sizes in terms of risk profile. However, there is a sense in which the West's asset managers are literally 'buying the world', since the total value of the funds they manage is roughly equal to total world GDP, which in 2008 amounted to $58.3 trillion (World Bank, 2011). Even more meaningfully, they are easily able to 'buy the developing world'. In 2009, the total GDP for all low- and middle-income countries amounted to $16.7 trillion, and in 2010 the total value of their stock market capitalization was $13.4 trillion, compared with the total of $54.7 trillion managed by the leading US and European asset managers (ibid.).

A great deal of discussion has taken place in the Western press about China's sovereign wealth funds, namely China Investment Corporation (CIC) and SAFE Investment Company (SIC), which are the principal vehicles for international equity investment by the Chinese government. Gerard Lyons, chief economist of Standard Chartered Bank, expressed widely held concerns:

> The big worry is that [sovereign wealth funds] see an opportunity to buy strategic stakes in key industries around the globe . . . [T]he expertise of emerging economies, such as China, in low cost manufacturing could quickly be added to by the acquisition of high tech firms overseas . . . If the West accepts that Chinese firms can buy freely overseas using state reserves then this should lead to pressure for China to open its domestic markets further. (Lyons, 2007)

China's sovereign wealth funds are estimated to have a total of around $700 billion of funds under management,[38] and they have made numerous minority equity investments in global companies.[39] In March 2011, the market capitalization of the two largest US companies, ExxonMobil and Apple, totalled $738 billion, roughly the same as the total estimated funds managed by CIC and SIC. In 2011 the market capitalization of the 160 US companies in the FT 500 amounted to $9.6 trillion and that of the top thirty-four UK companies in the FT 500 amounted to $2.1 trillion, totalling $11.7 trillion, which is seventeen times greater than the estimated combined funds managed by CIC

---

[38] There are numerous estimates, mostly of around the same level.
[39] The rationale for these investments and their performance is intensely debated in the Chinese press, with heavy public criticism when the fund managers have made losses on their investments.

and SIC. In 2010 the stock market capitalization of the high-income countries as a whole totalled $42.8 trillion (World Bank, 2011), sixty-one times as large as the total estimated funds managed by CIC and SIC. In other words, China's sovereign wealth funds cannot, under any circumstances, 'buy the world'.

Can China's national champion companies acquire, merge with and integrate global companies?

The culture of China's national champion firms is changing significantly, with intense efforts being made not only to raise technical management skills but also to deepen understanding of global culture. A new generation of business leaders is being trained in the skills needed to compete globally. Foreign-trained Chinese graduates are returning to take up positions in the national champion firms. The flotation of part of their equity has led to greatly increased media scrutiny of the firms both within and outside China. Remuneration practices have altered greatly. The appointment of international non-executive directors has deepened awareness of international business practice. As their international operations gradually increase, a new generation of Chinese business leaders is able steadily to deepen their understanding of the global economy through daily business experience.

However, 'going out' for China's large national champion firms is just beginning. They have limited experience of conducting international mergers and acquisitions. Although the share of international business is growing, most of the assets, employment, revenue and profits of China's national champion firms are derived from the large and fast-growing domestic market. Success in international mergers and acquisitions requires long experience and practice. The leading global companies make numerous acquisitions and divestitures annually. Skill in this area is a key aspect of their competitive advantage. Identifying potential targets and making a successful offer is just the beginning of a successful merger or acquisition.

There is still a significant gap between the operational system of China's large state-owned enterprises and the world's leading international companies. The management system is typically hierarchical, with innumerable layers between the lower and the higher levels. The methods of remuneration and promotion are still very different from those in global companies. At the higher levels, males are dominant, and there are only a handful of top women managers. There are few non-Chinese people in senior executive positions. These differences might make it difficult for China's large state-owned firms to integrate an international acquisition or to merge with a Western multinational company. However, up until this point, Chinese firms have had few opportunities to acquire or merge with significant multinational firms. The most significant example is Lenovo's acquisition of IBM's PC division. This appears to have been successful in terms of integrating the two entities, despite the wide apparent cultural difference. In 2007 China's ICBC acquired a 20 per cent equity stake in South Africa's Standard Bank for $4.5 billion. Standard Bank is the largest bank in Africa, and there appear to have been substantial mutual benefits from the relationship and no significant operational difficulties. These examples suggest that, if the high-income countries allowed them to do so, large Chinese firms might quickly learn to make substantial international acquisitions and integrate them successfully. Moreover, there are many examples of Western companies with substantial state ownership that have successfully acquired and integrated firms from other high-income countries, including the USA. Among them are EADS (France/Germany/Spain), EDF (France), Renault (France), SAFRAN (France), France Telecom (France), ENI (Italy), Finmeccanica (Italy), VW (Germany), Deutsche Telekom (Germany) and Statoil (Norway).

How open are Western governments to large acquisitions of and mergers with China's national champion companies?

The leaders of China's national champion firms are all appointed by the Communist Party, which still has a deep influence on the way in which the state-owned firms are run. Since the 1970s the party has changed greatly. China's leaders have made great efforts to upgrade the educational level and technical skills of party members and to deepen their understanding of the world economy, international relations and global culture. Despite these profound changes, there is deep political and ideological resistance among Western governments to permitting Chinese state-owned firms to acquire substantial assets through merger and acquisition, even though these firms are partially privatized and quoted on global stock markets. Western governments view China's national champion firms in a fundamentally different way from that in which they view companies from other Western countries with substantial state ownership. The idea that China can 'catch up' technologically by buying high-technology Western firms has so far proven to be incorrect. The main acquisitions by Chinese firms have been of loss-making companies in non-strategic industries, notably IBM's PC division and Ford's Volvo Car division. Both were small-scale acquisitions. The attempt failed at more substantial acquisitions in more sensitive sectors, by both state-owned and private firms, most notably that by CNOOC to acquire Unocal and the various efforts by Huawei to acquire small segments of the tel-ecoms equipment sector. Even the attempt by Chinalco to acquire a substantial minority stake in Rio Tinto was effectively blocked on political grounds.

4

The Complexity of 'Us' and 'Them': The Case of Strategic Industries

The complexities of understanding who 'we' are and who 'they' are may be further illustrated through examples from two industries of critical strategic importance, banks and commercial aircraft.

4.1 Banks

Global bank consolidation

The pursuit of power and income among top managers is a significant motive for mergers and acquisitions in the financial services industry. However, there is also a powerful industrial logic behind the pursuit of increased scale in this sector. Among these are economies of scope in relation to sharing knowledge across a global bank, made possible by the revolution in information technology, and providing an integrated service for global customers. There are also significant economies of scale, notably advantages in the procurement of information hardware and software; in marketing, with branding playing an increasing role in global bank competition; in risk spreading across business sectors and regions; in mergers and acquisitions, including skill in integrating acquired or merged entities; and in human resource acquisition, with large global firms attracting scarce talent from the global pool of top mathematicians and physicists. The giant global banks are the 'glue' that knits together the global business system. A large part of the financial operations of giant non-financial firms, including payrolls, taxes, hedging risk in foreign exchange and commodities, corporate finance and trade finance, typically is outsourced to global banks.

In less than a decade between 1997 and 2006, the top twenty-five banks increased their share of the total assets of the world's top 1,000 banks from 28 per cent to 41 per cent (*The Banker*, July 2006). In 2008–9, during the global financial crisis, there was an extraordinary spate of mergers and acquisitions among the leading banks from the high-income countries. JPMorgan Chase acquired both Bear Stearns and Washington Mutual; Bank of America acquired Merrill Lynch; Wells Fargo acquired Wachovia; BNP Paribas acquired the main part of Fortis; LloydsTSB acquired HBOS; Nomura and Barclays Capital divided Lehman Brothers between them; Commerzbank acquired Dresdner Bank; and Santander acquired ABN Amro's Latin American operations, as well as Abbey National and Bradford and Bingley. Following this, the share of the world's top twenty-five banks in the total assets of the top 1,000 banks increased to 45 per cent (*The Banker*, July 2009).

Asset management is a key driver of profit for many of the world's leading banks. In the asset management industry, the 'scale economies are harsh and unforgiving', giving large competitive advantages to the giant asset managers who can spend large amounts on IT systems. Total funds under management by the top 500 ('Global 500') asset managers rose from $25 trillion in 1997 to $62 trillion in 2009 (Towers Watson, 2010). The share of the top fifty asset managers rose from 52.5 per cent in 1997 to 61.7 per cent in 2009. None of these was from a developing country. US institutions managed 49 per cent of the total assets under management by the Global 500. In some segments of global banking, the degree of industrial concentration is even higher. In foreign exchange trading there is a total of $4,000 billion traded each day, and London accounts for 37 per cent of the total of this. The top ten banks, all global banks from the high-income countries, account for 77 per cent of the total traded in London (*Financial Times*, 1 September 2010).

Nowhere has the two-edged contradictory character of capitalism been more vividly illustrated than in the financial sector. The giant universal banks are at the core of globalization, 'knitting together' the global business system. The transformation of the financial system during the era of capitalist globalization has been truly revolutionary: 'In a single generation, our financial system has been transformed . . . into a highly concentrated oligopoly of enormous, diversified, integrated firms. This revolution has gone largely unnoticed' (Kaufman, 2009). However, the immense power and influence of giant global banks from developed countries was the central force in the liberalization of the financial sector in the developed countries under the Washington Consensus ideology. Regulatory capture and deregulation were the root causes of the asset bubble and credit expansion, which led directly to the financial crisis of 2008–9.[40]

Catching up with the leading global banks in international competition is an almost insurmountable challenge for 'national champion' state-owned banks that operate in protected markets in developing countries.

Global consolidation of IT suppliers

The IT revolution is at the heart of the transformation of global banking. Giant global banks each spend several billions of dollars on IT procurement, and intense pressure from the banks has helped to stimulate enormous structural change and technical progress in the IT industry. The banking sector is second only to the telecommunications industry as a market for the IT industry, and the global banks place enormous demands upon it to achieve technical progress. In recent years the IT industry has undergone a similar process of industrial consolidation as that in other sectors.

American firms stand at the core of the world's IT industry. The most visible sign of US dominance is the iPad, which has swept the world in recent months. The key innovator, Apple, has a 70 per cent global market

---

40 The history of the last three decades was anticipated by Marx over 100 years ago: 'Talk about centralisation! The credit system, which has its focus on the so-called national banks and the big money-lenders and usurers surrounding them, constitutes enormous centralisation, and gives to this class of parasites the fabulous power, not only to periodically despoil industrial capitalists, but also to interfere in actual production in a most dangerous manner – and this gang knows nothing about production and has nothing to do with it' (Marx, [1867] 1967, vol. 3: 544–5).

share, and its sales in China exceed those of Lenovo, the Chinese PC manufacturer. Apple's main rival in the 'tablet' market, Samsung, trails far behind. Other powerful rivals, including Sharp, HP and Dell, have all left the business. The pace of mergers and acquisitions in the IT sector continues at a frenetic pace, with US companies in the forefront. In the first eight months of 2011 alone, the largest deals in the sector all involved acquisitions by US firms: Google acquired Motorola Mobility (for $12.5 billion), HP acquired Autonomy (for $11 billion), Microsoft acquired Skype (for $8.5 billion), Texas Instruments acquired National Semiconductor (for $6.6 billion) and Applied Materials acquired Varian Semiconductor Equipment (for $5 billion).

The IT hardware and software sector has the largest R&D spending of any sector in the G1,400 (BIS, 2009). There is a total of 228 firms from this sector in the G1,400, of which three-fifths (134) are American. The R&D spending in this sector amounts to $139 billion, which is one-quarter of the total R&D spending of the G1,400. The IT software and computer services sub-sector has a total of sixty-nine firms, of which the top ten account for 74 per cent of the sub-sector's R&D spending. Eight of the top ten firms are American, including the industry's super-giants, Microsoft, IBM, Google and Oracle. The IT hardware sub-sector has a total of 159 firms, of which the top ten firms account for 46 per cent of the total spending. Five of the top ten firms are American (Intel, Cisco, Motorola, Hewlett-Packard and Qualcomm).

In the 1970s, apart from IBM, there were more than a dozen global mainframe manufacturers. Today, IBM has reached a position of complete dominance in the mainframe market, accounting for over nine-tenths of the total. Servers have taken over many of the functions that were formerly performed by mainframes. The server market for global banks is dominated by the giants of the world's IT industry, IBM and HP, which between them have around three-fifths of the global market. In 2008–9 their respective revenues were $95 billion and $114 billion, and their respective R&D spending was $6.0 billion and $3.5 billion (BIS, 2009).

Desktop software for global banks is a virtual monopoly for Microsoft, which has revenues of over $58 billion and spends over $9 billion annually on R&D. Business software for global banks is close to a duopoly, with Oracle and SAP accounting for around three-quarters of the global market. The huge cost of investment in R&D that is needed to remain competitive in this sector has driven most competitors out of the industry. Oracle has revenues of $24 billion and spends $2.8 billion on R&D (BIS, 2009). In recent years Oracle strengthened its already powerful position in business software through the acquisition of PeopleSoft (for $10.3 billion), BEA (for $8.5 billion), Sun (for $7.4 billion), Hyperion (for $3.3 billion) and I-flex (for $0.9 billion). I-flex is one of the biggest Indian software companies, with around 10,000 employees and a focus on business software for global banks. In 2007 SAP greatly strengthened its position in business software with its acquisition of Business Objects (for $6.7 billion). The main threat to Oracle and SAP arises from IBM's rapid advance in software and computer services through a series of acquisitions. The most important of these was its acquisition of the leading business software company Cognos in 2007 (for $5 billion).

The automated teller machine (ATM) has revolutionized the most basic and ubiquitous of banking operations. Three firms, NCR, Diebold and Wincor-Nixdorf, account for over 80 per cent of the market in ATMs for global banks. The ATM manufacturers have invested heavily in technical progress, including increased speed, modularized servicing and greater ease of use. Most ATM machines across the world use Intel processors and a high proportion use Microsoft software. Intel has revenues of over $38 billion and spends $5.7 billion on R&D (BIS, 2009).

Catching up with the leading suppliers of hardware and software to global banks is an almost insurmountable challenge for IT firms from developing countries.

China's banks

China has the world's two largest commercial banks in terms of market capitalization, and it has ten commercial banks in the FT 500, more even than its closest rival, the United States.[41] Few people predicted such a remarkable transformation in the global banking industry. China's state-owned banks have undergone a comprehensive transformation in the past decade. They have absorbed investment from foreign strategic partners, who have contributed their expertise to upgrading management systems. The management has undergone

---

[41] It should, however, be noted that the USA has a further twelve giant financial institutions which dominate the global list of 'financial service' firms in the FT 500.

a wide-ranging skill upgrading, including personnel exchange with giant global banking partners and intensive international training programmes. Flotation of part of the bank's equity on domestic and international stock markets has intensified media pressure on senior management.

However, the structure and operational mechanism of China's large banks is very different from that of giant global banks. The principal source of revenue for China's large banks is from lending to state-owned enterprises. The share of non-interest income is extremely small compared with that of global banks. Their international operations are very limited, and they have a minimal business in providing financial services for global customers outside China. The share of non-Chinese employees is extremely small. Chinese banks played no role whatsoever in the explosion of mergers and acquisitions in the international banking industry in 2008–9.

IT Systems of China's banks

Almost unnoticed, in recent years China's largest banks have quietly implemented a comprehensive and high-speed transformation of their IT systems. This involved enormous investment, but it contributed greatly to modernizing the banks' operational mechanism and helped to centralize risk control. Instead of the thirty to forty different hardware systems that they used to have, the main banks each unified their hardware into a single centralized system. From a negligible proportion ten years ago, over 60 per cent of the business of China's main banks is now conducted online. China's top banks now compare favourably with their global peers in terms of the sophistication of their IT systems.

IBM's mainframe computers are the first choice for China's 'Tier 1' state-owned banks, with a 100 per cent market share. The implementation of a huge programme of mainframe acquisition in China coincided with a step change in the capabilities of IBM's mainframe computers, which are steadily advancing in terms of the number of transactions they can undertake in a given period of time. The immense processing capacity of IBM's mainframes has enabled the consolidation of data processing in China's large banks into a single central data centre. Once giant customers have bought IBM's mainframes as the foundation of their data system, it is difficult to move to another system.

The market for servers in China's large banks is essentially a duopoly: shared between them, IBM and HP have over nine-tenths of the market.[42] The market for storage hardware in China's large banks is a duopoly between IBM and HDS (Hitachi Data Storage).[43] The core business software platforms for China's large 'Tier 1' as well as its 'Tier 2' banks are provided principally by Oracle, with SAP its closest competitor. China's main banks have invested heavily in the installation of a countrywide network of ATMs. These have greatly improved the ease and convenience for money withdrawals across

---

[42] Dell is also a powerful force in the overall Chinese server market. Dell estimates that, as a result of its deals with Chinese internet companies such as Tencent, 60 per cent of the Chinese internet runs on Dell servers (*Financial Times*, 19 September 2011).

[43] In 2009 Hitachi had annual revenues of $124 billion and invested $4.7 billion in R&D.

the country. Most ATMs are from one of the world's top three manufacturers – NCR, Diebold and Wincor Nixdorf.

In sum, giant US high-technology companies are deep inside the commanding heights of the most important of all strategic industries – the financial sector.

4.2 Commercial aircraft

Global consolidation of systems integrators

Large commercial aircraft and advanced military aerospace equipment contain some of the world's most advanced technologies. The design, assembly, marketing and upgrading of this equipment involves powerful economies of scale and scope. The design of a new aircraft requires enormous investments, with significant up-front costs during the launch stage. The industry has large economies of scale in procurement of components and sub-systems, as well as in aircraft assembly. Having a family of aircraft with common platforms enables the manufacturer to spread given R&D outlays over a larger number of aircraft and to achieve operating benefits for customers. A large installed base itself is the best demonstration of product reliability, operating efficiency and technology leadership.

A total of sixteen companies have produced large commercial jet aircraft at one time or another.[44] Since the

---

[44] These include Boeing, Lockheed, McDonnell Douglas, Airbus, de Havilland, Hawker Siddeley, Vickers, the British Aircraft Corporation, Sud-Aviation, VFW, Fokker, Tupolev, Antonov and Ilyushin.

early 1960s the size of the commercial aircraft industry has increased enormously.[45] Alongside the enormous increase in size of the industry, it has shrunk into a pure duopoly, consisting of Boeing and EADS, who compete ferociously. Boeing and EADS each emerged from a process of intensive mergers and acquisitions. They each have revenues of around $60 billion, and they each spend around $3.8 billion on R&D (BIS, 2009). In each of them the commercial aircraft division is closely connected with the military division. In 2009 Boeing's sales to the US government totalled $22 billion.

Catching up with the world's leading assemblers of large commercial aircraft is an almost insurmountable challenge for firms from developing countries.

Global consolidation of sub-system suppliers
Boeing and EADS each have procurement budgets in excess of $30 billion annually. They exert intense pressure on their suppliers to meet their demands in terms of technical progress and cost. Leading sub-systems suppliers work in intimate contact with the systems integrators to produce planes that are safer, more comfortable, more reliable, quieter and more fuel efficient. In order to meet the relentless pressure from the systems integrators, the major sub-system and key component suppliers themselves need to invest heavily in research and development and to expand in order to benefit from cost reduction through economies of scale and scope.

A powerful merger movement has taken place at all

---

[45] In the USA, the world's biggest market for commercial aircraft, the number of passenger miles flown rose from 33 trillion in 1960, at the dawn of the modern commercial airliner, to 584 trillion in 2008.

levels of the supply chain, and the level of concentration in the upper reaches of the aircraft industry supply chain has increased rapidly. A group of giant sub-systems integrators have established or strengthened their competitive position in businesses covering one or more aircraft sub-systems (see table 15). All of these suppliers, which are headquartered in developed countries, are global giants themselves, with billions of dollars in revenues and large R&D outlays. They dominate every major sub-system of the aircraft.

Engines are by far the most expensive aircraft sub-system, requiring enormous development costs and R&D outlays. There are now only three makers (GE, Rolls-Royce and United Technologies) that can produce large modern jet aircraft engines. Honeywell is by far the most powerful firm in the supply of avionics and related sub-systems. Both Goodrich and Rockwell Collins are strong competitors in the supply of avionics and other control systems. All three firms supply avionics and related sub-systems for both the Airbus A380 and Boeing B787. GE has emerged as the major competitor for Honeywell in avionics through its acquisition of Smiths Aerospace division, which it bought for $4.8 billion in 2007. Goodrich and SAFRAN are the world's leaders in the supply of landing gear and wheel and braking systems, supplying around three-quarters of the global market for large commercial aircraft. Liebherr is also a competitor.[46] SAFRAN is the world leader in

---

[46] Liebherr supplies the landing gear systems for Embraer's regional jets. It has revenues of around $10.4 billion and spends around $450 million annually on R&D (BIS, 2009).

Table 15 Revenue and R&D expenditure of leading aerospace sub-systems integrators, 2008–9

	R&D ($ million)	Revenue ($ billion)
Companies with a major share of		
revenue from aerospace:		
Finmeccanica (Italy)	2,400	18.5
United Technologies (USA)	1,770	40.4
of which: aerospace	–	24.5
SAFRAN (France)	847	14.8
Thales (France)	790	17.6
Rolls-Royce (UK)	705	13.1
Textron (USA)	475	14.8
Rockwell Collins (USA)	395	4.8
BAE Systems (UK)	306	24.0
Goodrich (USA)	267	7.1
B/E Aerospace (USA)	131	2.1
Companies with a minor share of		
revenue from aerospace:		
GKN (UK)	139	6.3
Toray (Japan)	506	18.2
General Electric (USA)	3,020	181.6
of which: aerospace	–	18.7
Honeywell (USA)	1,543	36.6
of which: aerospace	–	10.8
Mitsubishi Heavy Industries (Japan)	1,191	35.3
Kawasaki Heavy Industries (Japan)	400	16.6
Alcoa (USA)	246	28.1
Michelin (France)	693	22.8
Parker Hannifin (USA)	256	12.1
Liebherr (Switzerland)	459	10.4
IHI (Japan)	266	14.9
Eaton (USA)	417	15.4

All data converted to dollars at a rate of $1 = $1.438.
Source: BIS, 2009.

aircraft wiring systems and supplies the main part of the systems for both the A380 and the B787.

Even the smaller sub-systems on the large airplanes are dominated by a small number of powerful sub-systems integrators. Jamco is sole supplier to Boeing for aircraft lavatories. Meggitt supplies the fire and smoke detectors and B/E Aerospace and Recaro supply the seats for most large commercial aircraft. Many critically important components and materials are supplied by specialist aerospace divisions of giant global firms. Michelin, Goodyear and Bridgestone are the only firms capable of supplying tyres for large commercial aircraft. Saint-Gobain is the sole supplier of aircraft glass to Airbus. Alcoa is the world leader in the supply of aircraft rivets. Each A380 uses 2 million of Alcoa's titanium 'lockbolts'. Toray is the world's leading producer of carbon fibre, and it supplies most of the composites for the B787.

The leading sub-systems integrators in the commercial aerospace sector are immensely powerful companies, with economies of scope between their different divisions. They have each undergone large-scale merger and acquisition in order to consolidate their leading positions within the global aerospace industry. US high technology firms such as GE, United Technologies and Honeywell stand at the apex of this industry. In addition to their commercial aircraft sales, each has large sales to the US military, with close interconnection of the technologies.

GE GE's aviation division is part of the giant GE company. In 2008 GE had sales revenue of over $180 billion and spent over $3 billion on R&D. GE is the world's biggest aircraft leasing company (GECAS), with a fleet of nearly 2,000 commercial planes, and it has a massive financial division, GE Capital. It is a world leader in power equipment and medical equipment. In 2009 its aerospace division had sales revenue of $18.7 billion and employed 39,000 people. GE is one of the three giants that dominate the market for large commercial aircraft engines. Like its competitors, Rolls-Royce and Pratt & Whitney, it produces both military and commercial aircraft engines, with powerful economies of scope linking the two segments. In 2003–4 GE engines powered more than 80 per cent of coalition aircraft during Operation Iraqi Freedom. The company produces giant commercial aircraft engines, such as the GE90, which powers the Boeing 777, and its newly developed engine for the Boeing 787. Moreover, its 50:50 joint venture with France's SAFRAN (CFM) produces engines for around 75 per cent of the world's market for medium-sized single-aisle aircraft. It has supplied around 2,000 engines for Boeing's 737 series, 1,300 engines for the Airbus A318 to A321 series, and is the sole supplier for the A340 four-engine plane. The installed base for commercial jet engines produced by GE (including CFM) rose from 5,000 in 1990 to 23,000 in 2009. In 2009 GE's sales to the US government totalled $4.3 billion.

United Technologies United Technologies has total revenues of $53.2 billion and spends $1.8 billion on R&D (BIS, 2009). It Otis division is one of the world's leading manufacturer of elevators for tall buildings, along with Schindler, Mitsubishi and ThyssenKrupp.

Its Carrier division is one the world's leading manufacturers of cooling systems. However, its largest division is aerospace, with revenues in 2009 of $24.5 billion. It has three sub-divisions, Pratt & Whitney, Sikorsky, and Hamilton Sundstrand. Pratt & Whitney is the third member of the group of giant global aircraft engine manufacturers. It supplies engines for the Boeing B747, 757, 767 and 777 and for the Airbus A318 to 321 series, with more than 600 customers globally. For decades it has fought a 'Great Engine War' of intense duopolistic competition with GE to supply US military airplanes. Hamilton Sundstrand supplies a variety of sub-systems, including heating and cooling, cabin pressurization, ventilation control and flight control. Sikorsky is one of the world's leading manufacturers of helicopters. It supplies the US military with the Black Hawk helicopter, for which it has orders for 1,200 over the next twenty years. The US Navy's helicopters are entirely supplied by Sikorsky. It supplies nearly half of all the naval helicopters used by armed forces across the world. In September 2011 United Technologies made an all-cash offer of $18.4 billion to acquire Goodrich, which would further strengthen its leading position in aerospace. In 2009 the company's sales to the US government totalled $7.5 billion.

Honeywell Honeywell's aerospace division is located within a much larger high-technology company, which also produces automation and control solutions, specialist materials and transportation systems. There are powerful economies of scope among its different divisions. In 2008–9 its revenues were $31 billion and it spent

$1.5 billion on R&D (BIS, 2009). In 2009 Honeywell's aerospace division had sales revenue of $10.8 billion. It produces a wide range of aerospace products, including auxiliary power units, environmental control systems and electric power systems. However, it is by far the world's largest supplier of avionics sub-systems for commercial aircraft, producing flight safety systems, such as ground proximity warning systems and windshear detection systems, and communication, navigation and surveillance systems, such as navigation and guidance systems, global positioning systems and cockpit display systems. It supplies the core avionics systems for both the A380 and the B787. GE has emerged as the major competitor to Honeywell in avionics through its acquisition of Smiths Aerospace division, which it bought for $4.8 billion in 2007. In 2009 Honeywell's sales to the US military amounted to $2.9 billion.

Catching up with the world's leading sub-systems integrators in the aerospace industry is an almost insurmountable challenge for firms from developing countries.

Consolidation of China's systems integrators
In 1970 the Chinese government announced a project to build a large commercial airliner of the same size as the Boeing 707. The first Y-10 aircraft was completed in Shanghai in 1978 and made 130 test flights between 1980 and 1983. A total of two aircraft were built, one of which was tested to destruction on the ground. A dramatic newsreel exists of this process. It was a remarkable achievement for a developing country to produce such a technologically advanced product. The remaining

Y-10 can still be visited at COMAC's headquarters in Shanghai. In front of it is a sculpture with the characters 'never give up' (*yong bu fang qi*). However, the aircraft was not a commercial success and the programme was halted in 1985. Between 1986 and 1993 McDonnell Douglas assembled 34 MD 82/83 aircraft in Shanghai. In 1992 it was agreed that McDonnell and Aviation Industries of China (AVIC) would jointly produce in Shanghai 150 MD-90 commercial airliners using a substantial share of domestically produced components. In 1997, shortly after it had acquired McDonnell Douglas, Boeing announced that it was terminating the project. At this point just two of the MD-90s had been assembled. In 1996 AVIC and Airbus agreed a joint plan to design and produce a new commercial airliner, the AE100. Just two years later, Airbus decided that the proposal was not commercially viable and terminated the project without any planes having been produced. The termination of these two programmes set the Chinese commercial aircraft industry back many years. Since then China's fleet of large commercial aircraft has grown at great speed, consisting entirely of planes bought from Boeing and Airbus, which contest fiercely for market share in the country. It is estimated that between 2010 and 2030 China will purchase 3,800 large commercial aircraft, worth around $400 billion.

The State Council's Long-Term Programme for National Science and Technological Development (2006–2020) identified the development of large commercial aircraft as one of sixteen key areas for China's industrial development. The programme also identified enhancing indigenous innovation capability in the aircraft sector as an important part of the country's science and technology development objectives. The twelfth Five Year Plan (2011–15) emphasizes the development of high-end manufacturing industries. Large commercial aircraft embody a significant bundle of the world's most advanced technologies, including new materials, propulsion systems and information technology.

In the late 1990s AVIC was split into two separate branches in order to 'encourage competition', but in 2008 the two branches were merged once again into a single entity. AVIC is a vertically integrated entity that comprises all the main elements of the Chinese domestic aircraft industry, including aircraft design and manufacture – including both commercial and military – airframes, engines and avionics. In addition, AVIC produces a wide range of non-aerospace products, among them automobiles and auto components, gas turbines, refrigeration equipment and electrical goods, as well as being involved in service businesses such as aircraft leasing, transportation and health. It contains around 200 subsidiaries and thirty-one research institutes and employs around 400,000 people. In 2010 AVIC ranked number 330 in the Fortune 500, with revenues of $25 billion. In other words, the output of China's indigenous aircraft industry is roughly equivalent to the aerospace division of a single leading global sub-systems integrator such as United Technologies. The revenue of the world's top thirty-four aerospace and defence companies is over $500 billion and they spend over $21 billion on R&D (BIS, 2009).

At the same time that the two segments of AVIC were

merged into a single company, a new enterprise was established, the Commercial Aircraft Corporation of China (COMAC),[47] with the specific purpose of developing a large commercial aircraft, the C919. In 2002 the Chinese government initiated a plan to build its own domestically assembled regional jet, the ARJ21.[48] The consortium responsible for producing the plane was merged with COMAC in 2009.[49] The ARJ21, which is assembled by COMAC in Shanghai, had its maiden flight in November 2008, and by late 2010 there were over 200 orders, around three-quarters of which were from China's domestic airlines. The plane faces intense competition from Embraer (Brazil) and Bombardier (Canada), which constitute a duopoly within the global regional jet market.[50] The C919 will be a 160 to 170 seat plane that competes directly with Boeing's B737 and Airbus A320 in both domestic and international markets. It is planned that the maiden flight will take place in 2014 and the plane will enter service in 2016. In late 2010, COMAC announced it had received 100 orders.

---

[47] COMAC has its headquarters in Shanghai. Its principal shareholders are SASAC, the State-Owned Assets Supervision and Administration Commission, with 31.59 per cent, Shanghai municipal government's Shanghai Guosheng Company, with 26.33 per cent, and AVIC, with 26.33 per cent. Sinochem, Baosteel and Chinalco each have 5.25 per cent.

[48] The ARJ21 will initially have seventy to eighty seats. It is planned later to have a stretched version with ninety to a hundred seats.

[49] The consortium included several of the main subsidiaries of AVIC.

[50] The regional jet market is a small fraction of the large commercial aircraft market. It is predicted that the global market between 2011 and 2030 for large commercial jets (including single-aisle, twin-aisle and jumbo jets) will total over $4.0 trillion, while the market for regional jets will be just $70 billion – or less than 2 per cent of the total (*Financial Times*, 18 June 2011).

*The role of global sub-system suppliers in China's
aerospace industry*

Both the ARJ21 and the C919 use sub-systems from
the world's leading suppliers, with US firms at the
core of the supply chain, among them GE, United
Technologies, Honeywell, Rockwell Collins, Parker
Hannifin, Goodrich and Eaton.

GE's joint venture with SAFRAN – CFM – supplies
the engines for both the ARJ21 and the C919. The
ARJ21's flight deck, avionics, flight management and
collision-avoidance systems are supplied by Rockwell
Collins. SAFRAN supplies the flight deck control
system, Honeywell the fly-by-wire flight control system,
and Eaton Corporation the integrated cockpit panel
assemblies. Hamilton Sundstrand (United Technologies)
supplies the auxiliary power unit and the fully integrated engine and cabin fire protection system. Liebherr
supplies the landing gear, Goodrich the tyres and
brakes, and Parker Hannifin the hydraulic system and
the fuel control system. For the C919, GE supplies the
flight management system, including the core cockpit
computing system, cockpit displays and flight recorders;
Hamilton Sundstrand the electric power generation and
distribution systems and the integrated fire protection
system; Parker Hannifin the hydraulic system, the fuel
supply system, and the fly-by-wire flight control actua-
tion system; Eaton the fuel and hydraulic conveyance
system; and Honeywell the wheels, tyres and brakes, as
well as the starter-generators.

Through the ARJ21 and C919 programmes China
hopes that the domestic industry will catch up with the
global industry leaders in terms of systems engineering;

managing complex supply chains; advanced materials, such as composites and super alloys; advanced aero engines and other complex mechanical systems, including APU (auxiliary power units) and landing gear; certifying large commercial aircraft; and world-class customer support. However, the competitive challenge for state-owned AVIC is immense.

In sum, giant US high-technology firms are deep inside the most sensitive of all manufacturing sectors, the aircraft industry, in which military and civilian technologies are closely connected.

Conclusion

Is China buying the world?

Whatever the future may hold, it is far from the case today that China is buying the world. The statement 'China is buying the world' is powerful and emotive. A large body of the citizens of high-income countries appear to believe that this is the reality of China's relationship to the world in general and the rich countries in particular. Similar views were advanced in the 1980s in relation to the rise of Japan. However, the depth of feeling about China's rise greatly exceeds that of the 1980s in relation to Japan. The widely expressed view that China is buying the world is damaging to international relations, especially at a time of deep crisis in global political economy. It is damaging to the prospect for peace. It is important for the relationship between China and the Western world that there is balanced analysis of the relationship between large Chinese firms and the global business system. This requires a thorough investigation of the nature of capitalist glo-

132

Conclusion

balization and its implications both for ourselves and for China.

Who are we?

After the late 1970s China groped its way towards reform of its large state-owned enterprises and attempted to transform them into globally competitive giant firms. During the three decades since then, China's policy-makers have watched intently as global business entered an era of revolutionary transformation. During this period the capitalist business system went through comprehensive restructuring with explosive merger and acquisition at its core. In almost every sector there emerged a small group of giant companies with leading technologies and brands, which between them commanded 50 per cent or more of the global market in that sector. Pressure from the cascade effect stimulated comprehensive restructuring of the value chain surrounding core companies, and industrial concentration took place far down into the supply chain. This system has been tremendously dynamic, as ferocious oligopolistic competition has spurred unprecedented technical progress with tremendous benefits for society.[51] The same basic process of industrial concentration is at work in industries as different as automobiles and beverages.

During the three decades of capitalist globalization,

[51] Wild capitalist globalization has also caused profound contradictions in global political economy, in respect to the environment, inequality, the concentration of business power and the financial system (Nolan, 2009).

firms from high-income countries have enormously expanded their international operations. The international assets, employment and sales of leading global firms greatly exceed those within their home economies. They have, indeed, been 'buying the world' throughout this time. Firms from high-income countries have deeply penetrated each other's business systems, mainly through international mergers and acquisitions. A succession of iconic national companies in one high-income country have been sold to firms from other high-income countries. In the high-income countries, we can say to each other: 'I have you within me, and you have me within you'.

After three decades of capitalist globalization there is a tremendous disparity in business power between firms from high-income countries and those from developing countries. The companies that have established themselves at the core of the global business system almost all have their headquarters in the high-income countries. In the FT 500 there are wide swathes of business activity in which there are no firms at all from developing countries. Global brands and global technical progress are concentrated among a small number of firms from high-income countries that stand at the apex of the global business system. Firms from developing countries are almost entirely absent from the commanding heights of global technical progress. One hundred giant firms, all from the high-income countries, account for over three-fifths of the total R&D expenditure among the world's top 1,400 companies. They are the foundation of the world's technical progress in the era of capitalist globalization.

At the same time that 'our' firms have bought each other, they have become truly global. Not only have they deeply penetrated each other's business systems, they have also become deeply embedded in low- and middle-income economies as their markets opened under the influence of Washington Consensus policies. This brought many benefits to the societies, but it created a severe competitive challenge for local firms. Not only core systems integrators but also the leading segments of their supply chains have built their business systems in developing countries. Global firms, with their headquarters in the high-income countries, are increasingly 'inside' the developing countries, typically occupying commanding positions within their business structure in high value-added sectors. This poses a serious policy challenge for developing countries, and only a small number of firms have emerged to compete on the global stage with the leading firms from the high-income countries. Much of the widespread optimism about the possibilities for catch-up by firms from developing countries is based on the case of China and the perception that its firms are buying the world.

The fact that firms with their headquarters in high-income countries have been buying the world to construct global business systems poses complicated, severe and little-understood challenges for political economy in the high-income countries. The close identification of large corporations with the particular country in which they have their headquarters has greatly weakened. There is little incentive for a global company to contribute to a 'national industrial policy' if the home economy accounts for a small and declining share of the company's assets, employment and revenue. There is every incentive to minimize tax payments in the home economy and shift profits to a lower tax regime, and there is every incentive to move the company head-quarters to another country if the policy framework in the home country is considered to be problematic. Since the onset of the global financial crisis the economies of the high-income countries have stagnated, with high levels of unemployment, especially among young people and those with low skills. At the same time 'our' large firms have enjoyed buoyant sales and profits, thanks to the continued growth of their international operations, particularly in developing countries. Today's developing countries, with China at the forefront, will become an ever increasing part of the structure, inter-ests and culture of firms from the developed countries. Indeed, for many of 'our' leading global firms China is either already, or soon will be, the biggest market. As capitalist globalization continues in the decades ahead, these trends and the tensions they engender within the high-income countries are likely to intensify.

Who are they?

China's 'catch-up' has been one of the most remark-able aspects of the era of capitalist globalization. The 'Great Convergence' has transformed global politi-cal economy. Among the many remarkable aspects of China's transformation has been the emergence of a sizeable group of its state-owned companies among the ranks of Fortune 500 and FT 500 companies. In view of the extremely uneven nature of international business competition, it is unsurprising that China attempted to nurture 'national champion' firms through state-led industrial policy measures. In different ways, this is exactly what all of today's high-income countries did in the past, from the late eighteenth century onwards. China's national champion companies have made great progress in terms of institutional change and technical advance. The success of the country's industrial policy under the leadership of the Communist Party defied the predictions of almost all international experts.

However, although China has become the world's second largest economy, it is far from having caught up with the high-income countries. It is still a developing country with a low level of income per person and a population that is much larger than that of all the high-income countries combined. It faces great difficulties in moving away from the path dependence of its unbalanced and unsustainable growth model. China is unique in that it is moving out of the 'Lewis' phase of economic development with unlimited supplies of labour and becoming 'grey' while still a lower-middle-income country. It faces also heavy policy challenges to deal with the tremendous inequality in income and wealth that has emerged under the reform policies, to manage the pervasive environmental damage, and to move the economy away from heavy reliance on high levels of investment and rapid export growth.

China's relationship with developing countries has greatly expanded. Its imports of metals, minerals, oil and gas, and food have rapidly increased. Its developing country trade partners have considerably increased their imports of labour-intensive Chinese manufactures. China is a highly competitive supplier of a wide range of infrastructure facilities to developing countries. The fast expanding relationship in trade and infrastructure has produced tensions in its relationship with developing countries. However, the greatly expanded economic relationship with China has made an important contribution to accelerated development, especially in Africa and Latin America. In the high-technology and branded goods sectors for the middle classes of developing countries, and in the supply chain that surrounds these firms, large Chinese companies have made negligible inroads into the dominant position built up over many decades and now held in developing countries by multinationals from high-income countries.

China has a small share of the world's oil and gas reserves, and it is desperately short of oil and gas in relation to its extremely rapid growth of demand. It is widely thought that China is buying the world in relation to global supplies of oil and gas. In fact, nine-tenths of the world's oil and gas assets are not for sale, as they are owned by the NOCs. Moreover, after many decades of expanded international operations, Western oil companies have a dominant global position in those resources outside the control of the leading NOCs. The combined reserves of oil and gas in the hands of Western oil companies are several times larger than those held by China's oil companies. Western oil majors are also in a leading position in terms of the technologies and management skills needed to develop extensive and difficult sources of oil and gas. As late as the 1990s, China's oil companies had negligible international reserves. In the late 1990s Western oil companies went through an explosive round of merger and acquisition, including some of the biggest acquisitions ever completed in any sector. However, it is not politically feasible for China to increase its reserves and upgrade its technology through the acquisition of Western oil companies. Instead, China's oil companies have had painstakingly to build up their international reserves mainly through a sequence of small-scale acquisitions of minority positions in developing countries.

China is unique among large, latecomer developing countries in its degree of openness to international investment. A large body of leading global firms have 'gone into' China. That this should have happened under the leadership of the Communist Party is remarkable, and baffling to international experts. Multinational firms occupy key positions in large areas of the Chinese economy. They have been crucially important within China's exports and centrally important in the country's technical progress. Many leading multinationals from Europe and North America have each invested billions of dollars building their business systems within China, and each directly employs tens of thousands of people. Leading Western multinationals each have several billions of dollars of sales revenue annually in China. If employment in their supply chain is taken into account, then the numbers indirectly 'working for Western multinationals' there would be extremely large. Many leading Western multinationals source billions of dollars' worth of goods from China. In some cases hundreds of thousands of people are employed making the products exported to Western multinationals. The total sum of people in China who work directly or indirectly for international firms is beyond easy calculation. In sum, 'our' giant firms are deeply 'inside' China.

It is highly likely that China will continue in the attempt that it has sustained throughout its 'reform and opening up' to build a group of globally competitive large companies. However slow and painstaking the process might be, they will 'never give up' (*yong bu fang qi*). The main body of China's national champion firms are in a group of strategic industries, including banking, metals and mining, construction, electricity generation and distribution, transport, and telecoms services. They have been protected by the fact that they are state-owned. They benefit from state procurement policy and the fact that they buy each other's products. The non-financial firms benefit also from loans from state-owned banks. They have benefited greatly from the high-speed growth of the domestic economy.

However, expanding the position of state-owned national champion firms in a large and fast-growing domestic economy is different from constructing globally competitive firms in the international arena. Despite significant progress, China has not yet nurtured a group of globally competitive 'national champion' firms with leading global technologies and brands that can compete within the high-income countries. Despite widespread perceptions in the international media that Chinese firms are buying the world, their presence in the high-income countries is negligible. This is a remarkable situation for a country that is the world's largest exporter and its second largest economy and manufacturer. In other words, 'we' are inside 'them', but 'they' are not inside 'us'.

China was deeply scarred by the Asian financial crisis. Like other East Asian economies, it has accumulated large foreign exchange reserves, which it is widely believed to be using to buy the world. However, in per capita terms China's foreign exchange reserves are far below those of most of its neighbours, and it cannot simply use its foreign exchange reserves to buy the world. The primary function in accumulating large foreign exchange reserves was to protect the country from the risk of a global financial disaster – which erupted exactly as it had long predicted and feared – not as a weapon to buy the world. Accordingly, China's foreign reserves must be managed conservatively. The country's sovereign wealth funds manage only a part of its total foreign exchange reserves. Even if China wished to use these funds to acquire Western companies, they are small in comparison with the combined market capitalization of Western companies and are far from sufficient for China to buy the world. Moreover, there are severe political constraints on Chinese firms acquiring Western firms. Chinese firms have made only a small number of attempts to acquire significant Western companies, almost all of which failed. There have been only two significant acquisitions, and these have both been sales by a leading Western multinational of a low-margin, 'commercialized' division that it no longer wished to operate.

Conclusion

The complexity of catching up

The examples of China's banks and aircraft industry demonstrate just how severe is the challenge facing firms from developing countries. During the past three decades global banks have accumulated enormous technical and human capabilities, which enable them to function as the 'cement' that links together the entire global business system. In the past decade China's commercial banks have been transformed beyond the imagination of most people outside the country. However, they face a serious competitive challenge in international markets. A key part of that transformation involves the tremendous progress in the application of information technology. The key components of the transformation of the IT systems in China's banks have been supplied by the global giants of the IT industry, mainly with their headquarters in the United States.

It is a remarkable achievement for China to have built its own indigenous regional jet, and even more remarkable to be entering into direct competition with Boeing and Airbus in the market for large commercial aircraft. However, there remains a long and complicated battle to dislodge the world's leading systems integrators from their entrenched position within the world aircraft industry. Moreover, the sub-systems inside the ARJ21 and C919 are all from the global giants with their headquarters in the high-income countries, principally in the United States.

China understands fully the severity of the competitive challenge that it faces across the whole value chain on account of the process of industrial consolidation

142

and international expansion of business operations that has taken place among firms from the developed countries in the last three decades. China is attempting to build its own globally competitive 'systems integrator' firms. In order to achieve this it has opened its doors wide to leading global firms in the most sensitive of all industries – banks and aerospace. High-technology firms from the United States are at the forefront of this process, occupying leading positions deep within the value chain.

The question of who are 'we' and who are 'they' is far from resolved.

China has not yet bought the world and shows little sign of doing so in the near future.

References

BCG (Boston Consulting Group) (2009) *Wealth Markets in China*. Beijing: BCG.

BERR (Department for Business Enterprise and Regulatory Reform) (2008) *The 2008 R&D Scoreboard*. London: BERR.

BIS (Department for Business Innovation and Skills) (2009) *The 2009 R&D Scoreboard*. London: BIS.

BIS (Department for Business Innovation and Skills) (2010) *The 2010 R&D Scoreboard*. London: BIS.

BP (2011) *Statistical Review of World Energy*. London: BP.

Diamond, Jared M. (2005) *Collapse: How Societies Choose to Fail or Survive*. London: Allen Lane.

DTI (Department of Trade and Industry) (2007) *The 2007 R&D Scoreboard*. London: DTI.

Gao, Yuning (2011) *China as the Workshop of the World*. London: Routledge.

Halper, Stefan A. (2010) *Beijing Consensus: How China's Authoritarian Model Will Dominate the Twenty-First Century*. New York: Basic Books.

Huntington, Samuel P. (2005) *Who are We?* London: Free Press.

References

Hutton, Will (2007) *The Writing on the Wall: China and the West in the 21st Century*. London: Little, Brown.

IEA (International Energy Association) (2011) *Overseas Investment by China's National Oil Companies*. Paris: OECD.

Interbrand (2011) *Best Global Brands 2010*, available at www.interbrand.com/Libraries/Branding_Studies/BGB_Report_A4_Single.sflb.ashx (accessed October 2011).

Jacques, Martin (2009) *When China Rules the World: The Rise of the Middle Kingdom and the End of the Western World*. London: Allen Lane.

Kaufman, Henry (2009) *The Road to Financial Reformation*. Hoboken, NJ: John Wiley.

Lipton, David, and Jeffrey Sachs (1990) 'Privatization in Eastern Europe: The case of Poland', *Brookings Papers on Economic Activity*, 21(2): 239–342.

Luo, Xubei, and Nong Zhu (2008) *Rising Income Inequality in China: A Race to the Top*. World Bank Policy Research Working Paper no. 4700.

Lyons, Gerard (2007) *State Capitalism: The Rise of Sovereign Wealth Funds*. London: Standard Chartered Bank; available at http://banking.senate.gov/public/_files/111407_Lyons.pdf (accessed October 2011).

Marshall, Alfred ([1890] 1920) *Principles of Economics*. London: Macmillan.

Marx, Karl ([1867] 1967), *Capital*. New York: International.

Nolan, Peter (1995) *China's Rise, Russia's Fall*. Basingstoke: Macmillan.

Nolan, Peter (2001a) *China and the Global Business Revolution*. Basingstoke: Palgrave.

Nolan, Peter (2001b) *China and the Global Economy*. Basingstoke: Palgrave.

Nolan, Peter (2009) *Crossroads: The End of Wild Capitalism and the Future of Humanity*. London: Marshall Cavendish.

Nolan, Peter, Jin Zhang and Chunhang Liu (2007) *The Global Business Revolution and the Cascade Effect*. Basingstoke: Palgrave.

Nolan, Peter, Jin Zhang and Chunhang Liu (2008) 'The global business revolution and the cascade effect, and the challenge for firms from developing countries', *Cambridge Journal of Economics*, 32(1): 29–47.

Reich, Robert B. (1990) 'Who is us?', *Harvard Business Review*, January–February.

Reich, Robert B. (1991) 'Who is them?, *Harvard Business Review*, March–April.

SSB (State Statistical Bureau) (2000) *Chinese Statistical Yearbook*. Beijing: Chinese Statistical Publishing House.

SSB (State Statistical Bureau) (2010) *Chinese Statistical Yearbook*. Beijing: Chinese Statistical Publishing House.

Steinfeld, Edward S. (2010) *Playing our Game: Why China's Economic Rise Doesn't Threaten the West*. Oxford: Oxford University Press.

Subramaniam, Arvind (2011) *Eclipse: Living in the Shadow of China's Economic Dominance*. Washington, DC: Peter G. Peterson Institute for International Economics.

Towers Watson (2010) *The World's 500 Largest Asset Managers*, available at www.towerswatson.com/assets/pdf/2942/PI500-Analysis.pdf (accessed October 2011).

UNCTAD (United Nations Conference on Trade and Development) (2009) *World Investment Report*. Geneva: UNCTAD.

UNCTAD (United Nations Conference on Trade and Development) (2010) *World Investment Report*. Geneva: UNCTAD.

Wen, Jiabao (2010) Remarks by PRC Premier Wen Jiabao at a dinner in his honour hosted by the National Committee on US–China Relations and the US–China Business Council.

References

World Bank (2006) *World Development Indicators*. Washington, DC: World Bank.

World Bank (2010) *World Development Indicators*. Washington, DC: World Bank.

World Bank (2011) *World Development Indicators*. Washington, DC: World Bank.